Y0-CBI-673

THE VIOLENCE
OF OUR LIVES

The Courage of His Convictions

The Unknown Citizen

The Plough Boy

Five Women

A Man of Good Abilities

People of the Streets

The Twisting Lane: Some Sex Offenders

The Frying Pan: A Prison and Its Prisoners

In No Man's Land: Some Unmarried Mothers

*The Man Inside: An Anthology of
Prisoners' Writings* (ed.)

Three Television Plays

Lighthouse

*The People of Providence: A Housing Estate
and Some of Its Inhabitants*

Walrus: Three Television Plays for Schools

Soldier, Soldier

Red Hill: A Mining Community

A Place Called Bird (In Kansas, U.S.A.)

Life After Life: Interviews with Twelve Murderers

Russian Voices

May the Lord in His mercy be kind to Belfast

TONY PARKER

THE VIOLENCE OF OUR LIVES

INTERVIEWS WITH AMERICAN MURDERERS

An Owl Book
HENRY HOLT AND COMPANY
NEW YORK

Henry Holt and Company, Inc.
Publishers since 1866
115 West 18th Street
New York, New York 10011

Henry Holt® is a registered
trademark of Henry Holt and Company, Inc.

Library of Congress Cataloging-in-Publication Data
Parker, Tony.
The violence of our lives : interviews with American murderers/
Tony Parker.—1st ed.
p.   cm.
1. Prisoners—United States—Biography.   2. Murderers—United
States—Biography.   I. Title.
HV9468.P37   1995
364.1'523'092273—dc20   94-46146
[B]   CIP

ISBN 0-8050-3058-1
ISBN 0-8050-4957-6 (An Owl Book: pbk.)

Henry Holt books are available for special promotions and
premiums. For details contact: Director, Special Markets.

First published in hardcover in 1995 by
Henry Holt and Company, Inc.

First Owl Book Edition—1996

Designed by Francesca Belanger

Printed in the United States of America
All first editions are printed on acid-free paper.∞
1   3   5   7   9   10   8   6   4   2
1   3   5   7   9   10   8   6   4   2   (pbk.)

Grateful acknowledgment is made to the following for selections
used in this book:
Lines from *The Poetry of Robert Frost*, edited by Edward Connery
Lathem, published by Henry Holt and Company, New York.
"ygUDuh" is reprinted from *Complete Poems: 1904–1962* by E.
E. Cummings, edited by George J. Firmage, by permission of
Liveright Publishing Corporation. Copyright © 1944, 1972, 1991 by
the Trustees for the E. E. Cummings Trust.

FOR

ANTHONY STORR

LIFELONG FRIEND AND MENTOR

WITH AFFECTION AND THANKS

CONTENTS

V: THE VIOLENCE OF OUR LIVES
(FOUR MEN IN PRISON)

VI: VICTIMS

THE VIOLENCE
OF OUR LIVES

PREFACE

As Confucius or some similar traveler once remarked, "A journey of a thousand miles begins with but a single step." To write this book my own journey was considerably longer than a thousand miles, but the single step with which it began was a letter, which said, in part:

> I am an English writer and interviewer. Two years ago I published a book called *Life After Life*, which consisted of transcripts of tape-recorded conversations with twelve people, some in prison and some now out in the community on licence, who had committed murder and had served or were still serving sentences of life imprisonment as a result. I am now intending to put together a similar book of interviews with people in the United States of America who are in the same position. The criteria are the same:
>
> a) The person concerned should have, or have had, a life sentence for murder.
> b) He or she should agree that the finding of "guilty" was correct. (This will not be a book about innocent people who have been wrongly convicted, which is a different subject.)
> c) The person I talk to should be willing to have several hours' conversation with me in private, which I will tape-record, and there will be no other person present at any time.

In return I give the following assurances:

1) No other person but me will ever hear the tape recordings either now or in the future, and after I have finished with them they will be physically destroyed and incinerated.

2) I will not use in the text, or ever reveal to anyone else, the real name of the person interviewed. Nor will I say or indicate in any way in which American state the conversations took place nor—if the person concerned is still incarcerated—will I name the prison in which they occurred.

3) All references to actual place names, and the names of other people referred to, will be changed.

4) At the conclusion of each tape-recording session, I will ask the person I am talking to if he or she is worried about anything in the recording which might lead to identification: and if there is it will be erased then and there to the person concerned's satisfaction.

5) Neither the recorded tapes nor the text of its transcript will be submitted to any state judicial or penal authority for censorship, approval, or permission to publish.

From this the conclusion, I hope, is plain: talking to me will neither assist the person concerned in any way, nor be to his or her detriment. And, finally, there will be no financial inducement or reward.

Two hundred copies of the letter were sent to American organizations connected with offenders and ex-offenders, asking if they would approach possible contacts; to individual prisoners with whom I was already corresponding; to within prison organizations such as lifers-support groups; to parole and probation officers and offices; and to state prison authorities. The response was at first a trickle, then a flow, and eventually a flood of replies, just as when a stone is dropped in a pond it produces an ever-widening circle of ripples and waves.

As a result I made four visits to the North American continent, spending a total of five months there and traveling not one, but seven and a half thousand miles. I corresponded with and visited twenty-seven prisons: in each of them (with the exception of those in New Hampshire) I was given full and immediate cooperation, with little formality and complete freedom to talk to and make completely private tape-recorded conversations with anyone I chose. In all I carried out forty-three interviews lasting a total of one hundred and seventy hours.

The United States of America is a federation of individual states, each making its own laws, with its own criminal justice system and control of its own prisons (or "correctional facilities," as some states prefer to call them). There is also a federal system, but its prisons contain less than 5 percent of the total number of people incarcerated in the U.S.A.; and the procedures that have to be followed to be permitted access to them are so arcane and bureaucratic that I should probably now still be in America if I had once become enmeshed in them. Over 1.25 million people are in prison in America, more than half of them black or Hispanic. The United States has become the world leader in its rate of incarceration, having surpassed both South Africa and the former Soviet Union. Although in some respects its prisons are less rigorous than their English counterparts—visiting is permitted for much longer periods and far more frequently, access to outside-line telephones is more prevalent, correspondence is unrestricted and uncensored, and in some states postage for prisoners' letters is paid by the authorities—sentencing is more ferocious and punitive and for much longer periods than it is in most other countries. As is to be expected, this in no way reduces the amount of crime, either petty or serious, and gives no statistical support to those who proclaim its efficacy (any more than the use of the death penalty in those states that practice it reduces the murder rate).

The offenders and ex-offenders whose recorded conversations appear in this book are in no sense representative of American murderers. From so tiny a cross section no conclusions may be drawn, except perhaps a tentative reaffirmation of what William Penn the Quaker said, that there is probably if we can see it something of God in everyone.

T.P.

AUTHOR'S NOTE

My American publishers have omitted two interviews with prisoners who have not committed murder. Those interviews appear in the British edition, which is subtitled "Interviews with Life Sentence Prisoners in America."

I

THE FLOWERS THAT BLOOM IN THE SPRING

FOUR RELEASED MEN

TODAY'S THOUGHT
FOR TODAY

MUHAMMAD HUSSEIN

Hi there! This is the Student Admissions Office of the University of Calvinsville Plains. Greetings to you, whoever you are, this is Muhammad Hussein. I'm not here at my desk right now so please call back if you can, maybe a little after four. If you can't do that leave a message for me instead after the tone and I'll get back to you. It's a bright sunny day here without a cloud in the sky, and today's thought for today is there are two things to aim at in life: try your best to attain your goals, and while you're doing it enjoy the trying as much as you can. May your God be with you, and good-bye.

Massive and rotund, he was six feet four inches tall and weighed two hundred and forty pounds. Wearing voluminous red cotton trousers and a canary yellow sweatshirt, he sat with his feet up on his desk smiling, and his hands clasped lightly behind his head. His voice rumbled and chuckled while he talked. Groups of earnestly chattering students passed outside the window from time to time.

And man, if you'd ever seen me then when I was sitting at a bar chatting up this pretty girl who didn't come up as high as here on my chest, the thought'd never have crossed your mind. She had a neat little waist and a real good figure and big brown eyes, and she fluttered her long black eyelashes, know what I mean? And she'd giggle and flirt and poke me in the chest the way girls do, and anyone'd have taken us for a pair of turtledoves. She looked only a little bit older than me, five years at the most, not more. If anybody'd told you who she really was you'd have shook your head.

That she was my mother you'd just not've believed: but I was her very first child and she had me when she was thirteen. Then after me she had nineteen more, most by other men, I think there were five or six of them all told. When we used to go around together she was thirty or something like that: but she always kept herself looking so good you'd have had to have a long long look at her to guess her age. She was always good company too, I liked being with her: for all her troubles, I never knew her sorry for herself. She'd cough and she'd say "Oh Alan"—because that was my name those days—"Oh Alan I think I've fallen again, come on, take me some place I don't have to think about it yet a while."

Who my father was I never knew, but I'm not going to say any-thing not kind like I don't think my mother did either, because she wasn't like that even if some folk thought she was. It never worried me any and as far as I recall I never met him; but I did hear from my grandmother one time that he was a petty thief and had been in jail. My mother said she never married him because she wasn't the mar-rying sort: I think she did have a couple of husbands once, but one I was too young to remember and the other did nothing but drink and bet on the horses. There's not a lot else I remember about the early part of my childhood. Oh except for meatballs and spaghetti—that I'll never forget. We had it every meal every day, seven days a week, fifty-two weeks in the year. I think it was the only dish my mother knew how to cook, and I guess it was pretty cheap too with all those kids for her to feed.

We may have been poor but we were happy too: in the South Bronx everyone was the same so you didn't feel you were missing out. My family was so big, everybody seemed to be related to me. My mother had more brothers and sisters and uncles and aunties than I could count; I'd be talking with someone on the street and it'd be ten minutes before both of us'd realize we were cousins or he was my sister's boyfriend or something.

Not many kids bothered too much about going to school and their parents didn't either, since they'd been that way themselves when they were kids. The school people didn't seem to care greatly either about it; I don't recall ever getting into trouble for truanting. I never got into trouble about anything else either: now and again some of my friends were sent to juvenile correctional institutions for stealing or lighting fires in empty houses but I never was. I wasn't good but I wasn't bad, no worse than most kids my own age: mainly we all hung around the streets playing ball games and turning on fire hydrants when it was hot. My childhood was any ordinary black kid's childhood in a city: that's all, ordinary, full stop.

I had one big hero in my life. Every kid has to have one because he needs one, and this guy was mine. They called him Uncle Buckeye because he came originally from Ohio, only it was shortened usually to Uncle Buck. He really was my uncle, my mother's elder brother, not one of her live-in boyfriends: how he came to be living two blocks away from us I never knew. He had a lady friend he lived with who was a dancer: she was very beautiful and I guess she must have supported him because he never seemed to work. I'd meet him in the daytime in the summer and he'd take me on the ferry and buy me popcorn.

According to him, when he was younger he was a member of Joe Louis's training camp: he claimed he was a real close buddy of the Brown Bomber as Joe was called. The way he told it, Uncle Buck was the man who taught him how to knock out Jimmy Braddock and Max Schmeling and thereby remain undefeated heavyweight champion of the world, which he did and defended his title a record twenty-five times. I don't know whether it was true, I shouldn't think a word of it was. But it was marvelous to sit and listen to him telling it; he held me spellbound for hours with his tales. Another thing he said was he could have become a boxer himself if it hadn't been his misfortune to be born with brittle bones in his jaw—very brittle so that one punch there fractured them and so he could never be in with a chance. When I started growing in size he'd look at me with his head tilted sideways:

one day he felt my arms here like this and he said "You know Alan, before long I'm going to start training you up for the fight game, you could be very useful in the ring." Oh man, I'll never forget the look he gave me when I said I didn't want to be a boxer because I didn't like being hurt. I've always stayed interested in it though and that's because of him.

A good guy my uncle Buck was, very like my mother, everyone was his friend. He gave me good advice about lots of other things besides fighting that were useful: like how to sweet-talk the ladies, that was something I learned from him. "Treat them like you were a little bit shy of them" he said. "Let them be the ones who come on." That's been very useful to me all my life, I've found. I've never had trouble with ladies or from them either, and I've known several in my time: in fact I guess you could say they've been one of my chief delights. One of my biggest regrets is I couldn't have their company while I was in jail. I went in when I was eighteen and I came out when I was thirty-six. I mean, that's a long long time, right, to have to do without something you enjoy.

I'll tell you, in the five years since then I've tried hard to catch up on women but you can't be thinking about sex all the time, not every minute of the day and night. I mean I'd like to, but don't get me wrong: there's some kids here on campus it makes your head spin to look at them, they're such pretty girls. But I'm a grown-up man now, I've a job to do with money to earn and a wife and two little kids of my own to support. Well it's three kids actually, I've had one with another lady recently, about two months ago: and if it's yours naturally you've got to give a little financial support there, you can't go running off pretending it's nothing to do with you anymore. Besides she's a very nice lady, we have a good relationship, I like her a lot. She's very fond of me too, so it'd be a sad thing if we weren't to have nice times together anymore. Oh that time I spent incarcerated, it was a big waste of the best part of my life, there's a great lot of living I still have to do.

How I went inside was I murdered a guy, and I got sentenced to life. It was a bad thing and a sad thing, and it was kind of funny and ridiculous too that I'd get sent down for such a long time. I don't mean there's anything funny to laugh about, not in someone losing their life; whichever way you look at it that's terrible, everyone agrees. But I'd never been in any kind of trouble before with the law: so the first time was the last time, you know how I mean? Don't think I'm not sorry or ashamed about it, I am and I know I will be for the rest of my life. Only you can't help comparing yourself with other people and how things work out. There was a kid on my block called Danny who was the same age as me, our birthdays were both on the very same day: and if someone'd asked you which of us would end up in trouble, you'd have had to say him. Danny was always right into everything, over the top of his head. He took dope and he sold dope, and he dealt in it too: he did forgery and blackmail you could say on a daily basis, and there were a few protection schemes he ran on local shopkeepers as well. Naturally guns of course, he traded in those. And one or two kidnappings for ransom and everything else you could think of and some that you can't. But he never got caught. Everyone in the neighborhood knew what a nefarious character he was; whenever his name came up people'd shake their heads and prophesy he'd have a terrible end. But what happened instead? He kidnapped a rich white girl on Park Avenue and kept her prisoner and lived in an unused warehouse for three weeks down near the pier. And what does she do but fall completely in love with him and takes him off to Antigua or some other Caribbean island and buy them a place together. Last thing anyone hears of him he's living with her there in a big house with a pool and a luxury cruiser. And as far as anyone knows, that guy Danny's never done one day in jail in the whole of his life. I mean, man!

Anyway, so that's how it goes. I wouldn't bet that guy didn't kill some people either you know in his time. I killed one, and that was by accident. I'm not making excuses for myself, I did the worst crime of all: taking somebody's life away from them, you can't do worse than that. I paid not enough in some people's eyes, they think I should have been put to death for it or stayed in prison till I died. But I wasn't a criminal any other way: I didn't prey on society like Danny Savannah did: a menace to society like him, no way. I was stupid and irresponsible, that's the worst you could say.

I'll tell you how it came about, okay? I'd got me a new girlfriend and she was a real sweet kid she was: innocent, I think she was around fifteen. All my girlfriends were sweet though, and I can't just remember her name. Anyhow, she wanted for us to get married: not because she was pregnant or anything, just because she was serious with me and wanted me to be serious with her. Which I was, or anyway enough at least to contemplate the idea. I said that to her and she was so happy about it she wanted to take me to meet all her family; so I went to her home on a Sunday at her mother's invitation. She asked me to go over in the afternoon and we'd all have a great big meal. It was a brownstone house, a walk-up, and it had a nice yard in the back where we all sat around the table and ate because it was summer and hot. There was chicken and sweet potatoes and ice cream and beer, and about twenty people there I should think, her family was nearly as big as mine. They were all nice people, friendly people, and some of them were around me and this girl's age, and some of them older and had kids running around of their own. I remember it was a very happy day at first, everyone laughing and eating and drinking and some of them playing music and dancing and singing songs.

In the yard of the next house in the back there was another big family as well: they were sitting in the sunshine and partying too. Then after a while gradually, you know how it is, we all got together into one big amorphous kind of a group and you didn't know anymore which family was where: some of each were indoors smoking and some outside talking, everyone together and just having fun. But then things somehow started to go wrong: the littlest kids were quarreling over whose ice-cream soda was whose, who'd had more cookies than they did, that sort of thing, you know how kids are. Then one of them hit one of the others, then they all started pushing each other and falling on stones grazing their knees. Some began crying, one of the mothers told one of the others to keep her kid under control, and then their husbands joined into it and fists were raised. Before you knew what was what something like a riot had begun, and people were chasing each other through the houses, out of that one and into this one and running up and down everywhere. It was crazy it was, really crazy with everyone behaving that way.

Me not knowing where I was properly or who most of all the people were, I found my girl and told her we were leaving. I grabbed her by the arm and made towards one of the houses, I wanted to run out through it and get out that way into the street. She was yelling at me but I couldn't tell what it was, and I picked her up and put her over my shoulder, carrying her with her head down this way behind my back so's I couldn't really hear. She was trying to say to me I was headed towards the neighbors' house and not hers, and when I went in there were three or four guys there wanting to block my way. They couldn't see which girl it was I had hold of, so I guess they thought she was one of theirs and I was trying to abduct her. One of them pulled out a knife and he came at me swearing, telling me to put her down.

What happened after that, well most of it's a blur. My recollection's of trying to push past him in the hallway and one of the other guys wrapping his arms round my knees and bringing me down, and all of us ended up in a heap on the floor. The knife I remember though; I remember the knife clearest of all: it fell loose somehow and I picked it up and swung round with it. It went into the back of one of the guys who had fallen down with me and it was kind of odd because he didn't make a sound. He didn't move either: all he did was lay there facedown on the floor. Afterwards they told me the knife had gone straight through his ribs and into his heart. It was all so quick too: one minute there was a mass of struggling bodies all in a heap, then it seemed like only a couple of seconds later there was only me sitting on the floor in the empty hallway, and this guy lying next to me with the knife in his back. Everyone had run away somewhere as quick as they could, including my girl.

I stayed there like I was frozen, not moving or even trying to get up, all the time till the police came. It seemed like they arrived about one minute later, that's how I remember it but it can't have been as quick or anything like that. One of them stood holding his gun pointed at me and he kept saying "Okay now, don't move, hold it right there." I wasn't planning on doing anything different; I'd have gone on sitting right next to the guy's body while they took pictures of us, if only they'd known. I knew I'd killed him, that I certainly knew: but what to do about it or what came next I hadn't the slightest idea.

At my trial they made a big play about me being a brutal cold-blooded killer, how I'd stabbed this guy in the back when he was trying to run away from me, not even face-to-face to defend myself in a fight. When my attorney tried to argue it was the other way around, it was me who'd been trying to get away, the judge looked like he'd never heard something less believable in all his life. There was me not quite the size I am now but near it, and the victim no bigger than you are, I'm not meaning to be rude. My girl gave evidence for me that it'd all happened because I'd been trying to rescue her, but the judge paid no attention to that. It was like he thought she might be scared of me or something; he said to her "Don't be afraid."

Well though it's not for me to complain: I got a life sentence for homicide, but the guy I killed ended up dead with no life at all. That gets to me sometimes when I think about it; that there's nothing I can do to put it right, nothing at all. A guy I didn't know, about the same age as me too. Sometimes I try and tell myself he was the sort who carried a knife so that must say something about him, but lots of guys carry knives, it doesn't always mean they deserve to get themselves killed. That's bad whatever way you try and look at it man, you can't get away from that.

Say look it's twelve o'clock lunchtime already: what say we go to the campus cafeteria over there and grab ourselves some food?

Prison . . . what can you say about being incarcerated close on nineteen years? Not that it went like a flash: it sure didn't do that, it went like every day and every week of nineteen years. I never got into trouble there, not once. I think that was because of my size. That and the fact it soon got around I was in for murder, so no one felt they'd risk picking a fight. I didn't trouble the authorities, I did what I was told; whenever it looked like there might be trouble I went back to my cell and stayed there till it was over and done. What happened to pass the time mainly was visits from all my family: I had so many of them come to see me one of the guards said to me once I had more relatives than they had prisoners there. But it didn't mean I wasn't lonely, that was something I felt: outside there was a world and things going on in it and I couldn't take part, all of it was passing me by. I'd always a visit to look forward to from someone though, the next day or the one after that. Family and a whole lot of friends as well: and every one of them when they came kept up my spirits and wouldn't let me get down.

Never having gone to school much when I was younger, I did some catching up on my education as well. I went to evening classes and took courses in computer studies and office administration and a few other things, then I went on to ethics and philosophy. The end result of that was after ten years or so I changed the whole of my life. I'd never been a person for deep thinking before, I'd not even given much thought to anything else but having a good time. But a lady came to that prison once a week to teach a class in meditation, and that lady had the biggest influence on me of any person I've known. She was white and little and she had gray hair: she'd be around fifty or so. She had steel-rimmed reading glasses and they were always right here on the end of her nose.

She seemed to take to me somehow, and I sure took to her. We took to staying on talking together at the end of her class. She was a Quaker, only not a serious or solemn person at all; she was always ready with a joke and a laugh. She was a mighty clever woman, and she was very shrewd: there was something missing from my life and she knew that somehow and she tried to help me find out what it was. One time I made some remark to her, not a very serious one and I forget exactly what about, but I made some sort of a reference to God. She said to me "I've never heard you use that word before, who's your God?" I said I didn't have one, and she said but there was something of God in everyone, whether they recognized it or not. And the next week she brought in a booklet for me to read and it was called *What Quakers Believe.*

What was great about her was afterwards she never asked me had I read it, she waited for me to be the first to mention it again. And she didn't try to push the Quaker religion at me either: all she wanted it seemed was to open my mind. And she succeeded in it, because not long afterwards I started looking in the prison library for other religious books on my own. The one that appealed to me most was about the Islamic faith, and there was one or two guys around the place doing time who were Muslims so I started talking with them. Finally after a while I converted: I stopped using my given name Alan, and call myself Muhammad now like Muhammad Ali the boxer, to give witness and a sign. It's brought me a lot of inner contentment: after so many years in my youth being a drifting ship on the sea, it's like in the end I've come into port.

I owe it all to the old lady who started me on the journey, and now she's had another big influence on me as well. She moved on from the prison but when she did we kept up a regular correspondence, and after a time she joined the lecturing staff of this university. She discovered one of the things they did was a postal study course for long-term prisoners, leading to a diploma in psychology. She said if I was interested she thought it would be a good thing to try and do, specially when it came time for me to make application for parole. It's a four-year program, but when you're in prison you have latitude to stretch it out and do it at your own speed.

I enrolled, and everything she told me about it was true, including the influence it had with the board when it came to consider parole. It was very unusual—in fact it was almost unheard of—for someone to get permission to apply and be given it first time. But I did, and that was due to her entirely, and in writing the letter supporting my application she said as well when I came out they'd give me a job. That's the one I'm doing, it's assistant in the Department of Student Admissions. To say she's been a good friend to me, that doesn't near approximate to it, but she laughs and tells me I'm silly when I say to her like I do that she's my patron saint.

Like they should, everyone on campus knows I've done time and they know what it's for; that's how she said it should be and she was right. I walk around now knowing there's nothing I need be scared of for people to find out. That's a good feeling: it's nothing to be proud of that you've killed another human being, but people ought to know about it. And they should know that no matter how much time I did, I owe society a debt. It could be one day some kid related to the guy I killed might come here as a student, and I hope he'd feel if he did, I was doing the best I could to make it up.

Each semester I give a lecture to the students in the sociology faculty about what life in prison's like, the good things it does to people and the bad. There's not too many of the first in my opinion, but there's one point I try and always stress to them and what it is is this: I say you don't have to go to prison, nobody puts you there except yourself. We all know there are times the police frame people and the courts jail them for things they never did. But most people in prison did wrong, and it was their choice they were going to do it. And the word that's important there is choice: poverty, deprivation, lack of opportunity matter and they shouldn't be allowed, they should be fought against and not laid down under as though they'd been ordained. Least of all should you kill people if they won't come round to seeing things your way, or kill them because they don't give you what you want. That's what I tell them, and I think when they hear it coming from someone like me it makes an impact. Some of them ask me questions afterwards like did I really mean what I said, and would I extend it to include countries having wars with each other as well. And I tell them honestly yes I do, no nation should try to impose its will on another one. Muhammad Ali believed that too, that's why he wouldn't let them draft him at the time of the war in Vietnam.

What will I do in the future, what would I like to do? I've given it a lot of thought: most of all I'd like to finish my studies and get my final diploma, then I'd like to go home for a while to New York. My mother's getting to be nearly an old lady now: having all those children that she did, it wasn't good for her health. She still has her boyfriends though. The one she's lived with the last couple of years, he's a man who's good to her and kind, he looks after her well. But this lady here who's my wife, she's not so happy at the prospect of us living there: she says she thinks there's more chance in the big city of me getting into mischief, and I don't think she means crime.

But I'd like to go there for a serious reason too I would, and I'll tell you why. I want to work with youth if I can: boys' clubs, shelters for kids who've got no homes and are running round the streets and getting into bad ways. Chances are they'll turn to crime: they're the ones who need help, youngsters of that sort. Don't get me wrong but kids on campus here are mostly privileged ones: I can give them a talk about prison but the majority—their parents are looking out for them, they're sure of good jobs in the future, not like those who don't have their chances the same. When I'm finished here I'm going to see if I can get on an inner-city youth development project or something of that sort.

So man, there you are, that's the end of my tale. Any time you want help in meeting people out of prison you think might be interesting to talk to, call me up and leave a message for me if I'm not here, I'll be glad to do anything I can. Oh the answering machine, you like that and the thought? I'm pleased to hear it: someone gave me a desk calendar for New Year's, there's a new quote on it for each day. Any time I'm going out some place I record it for people to hear, it makes them laugh. And you know what one guy said last week to me when I picked up the phone? He said "Get off the line Muhammad, I don't want to talk to you, I've only called to hear the message for today." I thought Well, I'll be doggoned.

A VERY CURIOUS

EXPERIENCE

LEE NEWMAN

*T*o avoid the blistering sunlight beating through the kitchen window of his cramped and dingily furnished apartment, he sat on
a stool with his back to a side wall, sipping from a can of beer
while he talked. He had sparse receding hair and dull blue eyes. His voice
was hoarse, his lips crookedly aligned, and his cheek under one eye socket
was disfigured and scarred: years before, he had been shot in the face.

I'm a forty-eight-year-old man and I came out of jail five weeks
ago: I'd been inside twenty-six years. And you know what I never
expected? That when I came out I'd feel real lonely. But I really do.
Inside you never think the only people you know are all either con-
victs or guards: so once you get out you don't recognize anyone,
there's not a single person whose face you know at all. I was in a coffee
bar one day last week and the guy sitting at the next table, he looked
kind of familiar: I wanted to lean over all of a sudden and say, "Excuse
me pal, weren't you in Attica one time?" Then just in time I realized
no, he wasn't who I'd thought. Well I'll get over it gradually I guess,
least I hope so, otherwise I'll have been too much institutionalized.

About myself, I guess there's not much to say. I'm a criminal,
that's all. Did you ever hear of Angela Davis, the Black Power movement woman? A year or so ago she was on the radio, I just happened
to drop in on her and she was saying prison defines criminalization all
the way and all the time. If you and me both committed the same
offense, a small one, you'd be fined because you've no previous form.

15

But as for me, I'd probably be put back inside because I've a record and I'm therefore a criminal. Another thing I remember, I thought what she said was right: she said going to prison defined your chances of future criminality too. After it you either didn't do what had got you there anymore, or it made no difference at all to you and from then on you went the same way only worse. I liked that, I thought she knew what she was talking about.

I'd go along with it, it was definitely true for me. I was a robber from when I was around sixteen and prison confirmed it for me. The first time I went away I decided straight off I wasn't going to stop. All I wanted to do was get better at it and not get so easily caught. My parents never understood it at all: when they came to see me they used to say things like "We hope you've learned your lesson." Well I had, but it was the opposite to what they had in mind. I was the eldest of five—three girls and then another boy—and none of them followed along the same path I did. So maybe what happened to me taught them a lesson even if it didn't work as far as I was concerned.

Why I was a robber, why I decided to be one, I honestly don't know and I never have. My family weren't poor so it was nothing of that sort: as a matter of fact my father did well for himself, he was always hardworking and he eventually became a furniture departmental manager for a big store. We had a big house, two cars, vacations at our lakeside cabin in the Adirondacks, all that kind of thing: and my parents really liked each other and got on together, which was quite something even for these days. I did okay with my schooling too: I wasn't brilliant, but I got by. So I can't throw light on why things turned out as they did. I used to try and puzzle it out once upon a time but that was years ago: in the end I gave up because I never could. Basically I guess it might have been because I was bored with middle-class life. I think excitement's often a reason people take to crime: they do it for that rather than financial rewards. In my time I've met a lot of guys inside like that: the only thing that ever animates them is talking about crime. A kind of light goes on in their eyes and you know all they're waiting for is to get out and get back into it again. Something else people don't understand either is how a lot of women quite like that too in a man: they're not criminals themselves, but hanging around guys who are, specially ones who are supposed to be a bit dangerous, it seems to give them some kind of a buzz.

The first proper kind of robbery I ever did was as a sort of test for me by an older guy: I was sixteen and he was twenty-one. For some reason I was fascinated by him when we'd been at the same high school: when he left he set up a delivery business with a little van and he used to run around town in it. But mostly that was just a front: he had a reputation of being leader of a gang who did filling station stick-ups. When I asked him about it straight out one time he just laughed and told me not to believe everything I heard. But I went on trying to talk with him every opportunity I could: I was envious of him because he always had plenty of girls around him, and at that age I was too shy even to talk with girls most of the time.

One night I told him I'd be interested in pulling a job if one was going, and asked him could he put me on to something. He said no at first, but a couple of weeks later he started questioning me about had I ever done anything with anyone else. I had to tell him I'd never done anything at all but I wanted to learn. It sounds a naive way to get into crime, but that's how it was. At first he said he didn't know of anything, but eventually because I kept on and on asking him, in the end he said the most important thing first for everyone to know, including me, was how well I could handle myself. He thought maybe he could arrange it for me to meet a friend he had who'd perhaps fix something to try me out on. And when the meeting took place a few evenings later in a local diner, I had a big shock: the guy I was introduced to was about the same age as me, that was all. From what he said and how he said it, it was obvious he was fairly experienced though, and we arranged we'd meet a week later and he'd meantime sort something out.

He came up with the idea I should rob a taxi driver, but I had to set it up and carry it out entirely on my own except for backup at the end. I decided I'd go to the local railroad station one evening after it was dark, and then come out of there like I'd just come off a train. Outside I'd take a taxi and say I wanted to go some small place out in the country; then when we got there I'd pull a gun on the driver and take his money. The young guy agreed he'd meet me at the station and give me a gun and after the robbery he'd come driving along and I'd jump in his car and he'd drive me away.

The funny thing was for the two or three days before I was to do it, I wasn't nervous—not at all. I was looking forward to it and keen I'd carry it out successfully, because I knew it was like an exam, something I had to pass before I could properly start on a life of crime.

And except for one small thing, it all went off smoothly and in every way okay. I collected the gun from the guy on the station platform where I met him as a train was pulling in, then I walked out to the plaza at the front. I took the first available taxi and told the driver the name of the village in the country where I'd worked out to go, which was about ten miles out of town. On the way there I chatted with him about this and that and I still wasn't nervous, so he had no idea he was being set up. When we arrived at the place I said I was going to I asked him to pull over by some trees opposite the gate of a farm. When he did I got out of the taxi and went round to the window at his side and held my money out so he'd have to wind it down. As soon as he did I pointed the gun at his head and ordered him out. Then I told him to empty his wallet and throw all the money in it on the ground.

That was my small mistake, because I told him to back off while I picked it up, and then I told him to get back in the taxi and drive away fast. It was no great surprise that he did: most of his money of course was either in his pockets or under his driving seat, while the money in his wallet wasn't more than around sixty dollars.

Well that's how you learn said the guy who came up behind in the stolen car for me like we'd arranged: the important thing was I'd carried out the stick-up okay, and all on my own. I'd kept cool all the way through, and that meant I was someone who would be known as reliable from then on for future consideration. I was in, and the only difference between me and a college graduate was I didn't advertise it by putting letters after my name.

A couple of weeks after that I was offered to join with some others on a bigger job. I think it was to stick up an all-night grocery store or some place like that, and from then on I learned about advance planning and that kind of thing. That side of it's just as important as doing the actual job itself, or maybe even more: how you have to keep watch on a place maybe a whole week before you hit it, to work out the best time to go in when the least number of customers are there. You find out what security they have, what sort of alarm system there is, where they put the cash when they empty the till, when's the least number of staff there on duty: every detail about it all that you can find out. Like you start any other job, if you're going in for robbery you start by learning what there is you've got to learn. I was never a big-time robber because that was something else I learned too: you don't have to be. You can make a steady living a long time if you don't get big ideas and try things out of your class. A headline in small print near the bottom of the local newspaper's inside pages is better than big print on the front with lots of pictures that'll bring everyone looking for you. It's better to be content with less publicity and just get along.

Oh my God this heat's really something this summer, isn't it? Let's take a break shall we, I'll go down the corner and get us some more beer.

I went on quite a few years the way I was saying. But I'd not been getting along too good with my family for a while, so I moved out of my home and set up my own place the other side of town. I was going steady with a girl who was Puerto Rican: her name was Anne-Marie. My family didn't like me associating with what they called "coloreds"; they thought white folk should stay with their own kind. I'd dropped out of high school and they thought this girl was somehow responsible for it. Which she wasn't, she was at school herself, but her parents broke up and she wasn't happy living with either of them, so she decided she'd move in with me. I don't think she knew how I made my living but she didn't ask: she came from a background where women don't question their men and it didn't worry her I never said anything much about myself. That was something else I learned: if you don't tell people things there's nothing they can pass on about you if anybody starts to question them. I've met lots of guys in prison in my time who were there as a result of what their women had told the police about them; often it was after they'd split up and the women wanted to get back at them and do them harm. Those guys never wised up either: in prison they were always boasting about things they'd done but hadn't been caught for yet. The way I see it that's just plain dumb. Anne-Marie didn't ask, and I never told, and I think that's the way it should always be.

I guess she was surprised quite a lot about how much I'd done when I finally got caught. She came to see me in jail before my trial came up, and a thing I liked about her a whole lot was she didn't say she'd wait for me until I got out of prison; she said she knew and I knew for both of us it had to be good-bye. She was a great girl, absolutely straight about it: I've never met anyone else like that in the whole of my life since then. I've thought sometimes if I could go back and start over on things I'd stay living on my own with someone like her.

It was until I was nearly twenty I guess that things had gone on okay. But when in the end I was caught it was my own fault because several things happened which I shouldn't have let happen at all. I did a hit with four others, and five's too many any way you look at it; someone's going to be the link in the chain that breaks down. And that's just how it was. I should have known better from the start not to join up with people I didn't properly know.

There was a filling station job to be done in Arizona and I was invited in on it because a guy had been taken sick and the gang was one short. They said all the beforehand planning had been done, and I spent a couple of days with the guys who'd set it up, looking round the area and reconnoitering the best route for getting away. There was a diagram of the actual place to be hit, and it'd been decided to use two cars. We were going to go in at two o'clock on a Wednesday morning because that was the one night in the week a security van didn't come and pick up the day's takings. The diagram showed the exact location of the safe where the money would be put, and guns and masks and false license plates for our cars had all been arranged. At first sight everything seemed to have been covered, including where the alarm button was clearly marked, underneath and to the right of the cash till. But I remember having the feeling something wasn't quite right: and if you get that feeling when you're the boss, or you're thinking of doing a job on your own, you don't go ahead with it. You go by your instincts always, and the more you're experienced, the more attention to them you pay. But in that setup I was an outsider, and against my better judgment I let it ride. A big sum of money was involved, and I didn't follow the rule about possible publicity: I'd made a two-day trip to Arizona, so I decided on balance to take a risk, which was bad.

When we went in, everybody knew what their exact responsibility was: mine in particular was to see nobody got to anywhere near the alarm. There were only two guys working there, and at first everything seemed to go nice and smooth: we had them backed up round the storeroom shelving out of sight before they knew what was happening to them. When we told them to open the safe one of them took the keys out from his pocket and without any argument he did everything we said. It all went too easily; looking back anyone could see that. There was a lot of money in the safe when they opened it, almost more than we could put into the bags for it we'd brought: a couple of the guys were grinning themselves silly because they thought we were having so easy a ride.

We were. It was so easy even if none of the others did, I should have known why. We'd walked straight into a trap: there'd been a tip-off, maybe from the guy who'd dropped out sick. He'd be the obvious one though we never found out. On the strength of it the police were staking out the place two hours at least before we arrived. There was none of that cars speeding up with sirens wailing and armed men jumping out like you see in the movies, nothing like that: just complete silence till we came out in the back. Then a wall of ten or twelve of them all switched their headlights on simultaneously and a couple of voices shouted at us through bullhorns to throw down our guns. They let off a few warning shots in the air too, to make the situation exactly clear what would happen if we didn't comply. At times like that you can be a hero if you want: but you'll be a dead one, that's for sure. So there it was: a real good botch of a job, and nothing to look forward to after it but a long stretch for armed robbery.

I drew a sentence of ten to twenty years, and it wasn't a prospect I looked forward to in any way, being incarcerated for that length of time. All of the first year inside I spent every day and night thinking nothing else but how I could get out. If you want to do that it's necessary to have some knowledge about the place you're in and how long you'll be there in that particular prison before they move you on to some place else, and just when that'll be, and how. And mostly you're on your own about it: despite the impression the media likes to give about it that prisons are full of raving gorillas wanting to get loose, most guys inside accept they're there for whatever number of years their sentence is and the majority decide to make the best of it. If that wasn't true there'd have to be six times the number of guards there are to keep them held down. Most guys would walk out if someone left the gate open by mistake, but mainly they cooperate in their own imprisonment.

I wasn't one though, not then; I didn't accept the idea of being in prison at all. I found another guy who felt the same way, and we worked on an old-timer who was in forever: the authorities trusted him enough to let him be in the administration office. With a mixture of threats and bribery we persuaded him to give us advance information about an upcoming transfer of twenty inmates including us to another correctional facility due to be carried out in a couple of months' time. A few days before the exact date of it we both went sick so we'd miss it: which meant they had to take the two of us on our own a week later on a separate trip in an armored van.

The complement was five: me and the other guy with an armed deputy sheriff who was the driver and two armed prison guards. We were cuffed to them, one of us to each, and I'll not be specific about how it came about but the other prisoner and me both had guns too, though naturally that wasn't something known. Three hours or so along the highway we made a stop at a rest station, and when we got back to the van before the cuffs were put on us again, that was our chance. The shooting started and it lasted maybe a minute, that's all: the end result of it was there were two dead and three who survived. I was in the latter category obviously, otherwise I wouldn't be here now talking to you, but the other prisoner wasn't lucky; he was killed and so was one of the guards. The deputy sheriff put his gun right on my face and tried to blow my head off: that's how I got to be this way with my mouth and cheek and my vocal cords. But I was lucky that I didn't actually die I guess.

They had me in the prison hospital a whole year afterwards for repair surgery before they could bring me to trial, and when they did I knew what I'd get, which was sentenced to death. I hadn't expected any other outcome, so it wasn't a surprise. I was on death row a month short of three years waiting to go to the electric chair.

How was the train trip this time? Yeah, right, the heat's dropped a bit this week. Christ, I hate it when it's so hot without a break. Want something to eat? Sure—only a beer?

Well death row then . . . let's say it's a very curious experience. I learned a lot about myself when I was on it, at least I think I did. To each person it's different; a lot depends on someone's individual makeup how they react. To me there was nothing particularly frightening about it: I never really believed I was actually going to die. Only when you come to think about it afterwards you realize it might truly have happened. While you're there you never fully get hold of the idea in your heart; you can't grasp the concept that one day someone could come along and legally put you to death. Mainly it's because you're busy all the time thinking about appeals. You read your trial transcript over and over, have long discussions about every detail in it with your attorney, and between you you decide which avenue you'll go along first. You'll maybe find as many as six different points as possible grounds: but you don't put them all in at once, you take each one separately and draw it out as long as possible.

That occupies your thinking entirely: first you argue reason A why they can't execute you; then at the end of the line with that one if it finally fails, you start again with reason B and follow the whole process right through with that one. Then the same for C and D and E: you've got each one lined up ready to put forward when the one before it fails. That makes sure you've all the time got something to think about and hope about: that there'll be some new flaw you discover in the evidence. And there's always the possibility if you spin it out long enough that there'll be some slight change in the law that'll give you different new grounds again to make another appeal. When you hear of guys doing big long fixed sentences that mean they'll never get out and who've nothing to live for because the future doesn't exist, you're not like they are: with a death sentence you're never in their position, you've always something to hope about.

In the prison I was in, death row was the gallery on the top landing of the six-floor block. There were fifteen cells, and they had twelve blacks there, two Hispanics, and one white man which was me. The blacks kept themselves to themselves and the Hispanics spoke Spanish all the time: I didn't have anyone much to talk to so I read a lot instead and that started a habit I've had ever since. My family were pretty good: my parents came to see me and my sisters did and they all kept sending me a regular flow of books and magazines. That was the first time in my life I got into reading: I started with fiction, but not a lot of it appealed; I found philosophy more to my taste. In particular I went into existentialism: that was very fashionable around that time. I read Sartre and Marcuse and people like that, and Camus made a big impression on me too, I remember.

But for me the best thing of all was discovering poetry, especially some of the moderns. I'd never read any before and if you told me two years earlier I'd be reading T. S. Eliot and W. H. Auden, I'd probably have asked you which jail they were in, for how long and what they'd done to get there. A few of them seemed right on my wavelength, or I ought to say I was on theirs. One I specially liked was Auden. There was a poem of his in a magazine I liked so much I tore it out and fixed it up on the wall of my cell. It was called "Aubade"; eventually I found out that meant a kind of song to be sung at dawn. I don't remember properly how it went, but part of it said something like "We are free to choose our paths, but choose we must, no matter where they lead." It goes on—"Time is a city where each inhabitant has a political duty nobody else can perform"—and it ends "Listen mortals, lest ye die." In the circumstances I was in when I read it it had a lot of meaning for me. It's difficult to explain but I somehow felt it had been written for me personally, and it had been written to other people as well, on my behalf. I kept reading it out loud and hoping someone'd hear.

Eventually they did, or that's the way I like to think it was, because after I'd been nearly three years on death row my sentence was commuted. It had nothing to do with my appeals, it was all down to the gubernatorial system: there was an election and a new state governor came in. One of the first actions he took was he granted an amnesty to everyone waiting to be executed because he didn't agree with the death penalty. My sentence was changed to life imprisonment like everyone else's, with even eventually a chance of parole, so for a second time I was again a lucky guy.

The reading habit I'd got into, which had led me to thinking about the meaning of life and all that, and the commutation of my death sentence—altogether they had the effect of bringing about quite a big change in me and specially because of the fact that after a time there might be a chance of parole. If that thought hadn't been there and it'd just been a life sentence forever, things would have been different, but since the possibility at least existed, I started to think maybe I could accept doing time. That idea had never even entered my mind before so it was a new and novel sort of thought.

I didn't make a quick decision, but I started to try and look at it logically and I came to the conclusion that if I decided to try and break out again, either I'd get myself killed in the attempt or if I did make it, I'd be a much wanted man forever and there'd never be anything else but a life on the run. If I stayed where I was though and didn't let myself be too institutionalized, on balance that would be more sensible. So I decided I'd stay where I was and do my time. And maybe if I could I'd put it to some kind of use as well.

I'm not an academic sort and self-education in a formal sense didn't much appeal: there are guys who enroll for courses and end up with diplomas and certificates or even degrees, but I wasn't that sort. It seemed too restrictive and leading to a way of thinking that'd be very conformist and bland. I wanted to keep myself alive inside my head, even if it did look on the outside like I was becoming compliant and toeing the line. I worked out a scheme I thought would be a good pattern for a way of living in incarceration, and all the time I was inside I followed it through.

I had something like what might be called a long-term curriculum, sections of studying things as deeply as I could for a couple of years each. First I spent all my time reading the great classics of literature: Shakespeare, Dickens, George Eliot, everyone. Then for the next two years I concentrated on art: I studied reproductions of things by all the great masters from Renaissance times through to the Pre-Raphaelites and Picasso and Modigliani and so on. I followed that up studying world religions a couple of years. Christianity, Buddhism, Confucianism and the rest. Then I went on to political history and followed that with modern drama, plays by Arthur Miller and Beckett and people like that. After that again I took up another different subject, then another, and one more again after that. It sounds a strange thing to say about being in prison a long time but I did, I enjoyed it: being locked up opened a lot of doors which I'd never known were there before.

One of the best things about it was it helped me keep myself to myself. I'm not a person makes friends easily, so living that way wasn't difficult. I never had deep long conversations with people, or struck up lasting relationships of any kind. I didn't want to—one sure way of being institutionalized is having conversations all the time with other people who are in prison like you are. You get swallowed up by prison culture and its talk and way of life. All you've got of your own is your own mind: you have to protect that and not let it be swamped by what's around you everywhere. As far as your parole applications go you have to think of them as irrelevant: with the sentence I had I knew I'd no chance of being paroled for twenty years. As a matter of fact it got well past that time but I knew it'd come one day. When it finally did my only feeling was one of slight surprise, and I haven't got over it yet.

To be frank, I'm apprehensive too, I'm not sure how I'm going to survive or what I'm going to do. My parents have both died: six years ago my father, and my mother not long after him. My sisters are all married and living their own lives; one's in Europe, one's in Australia, and the other's in California. I don't know where my brother is, we've had no contact between us in years. I suppose I'll look for some kind of job somewhere: maybe I'll be lucky a third time and find something good. I don't think that's likely somehow, but who knows? One thing I learned in prison was patience so I'll wait and see. My ambitions aren't very big and they aren't of the sort now that would cause anybody hurt; I mean I'd not kill for them or even steal anymore either, at least I don't think I would. I'm not sure about it though: maybe Angela Davis was right, prison criminalizes you for good. A guy last week offered me a gun. There was quite a temptation for me about it for a minute. Are you interested yourself in it? Some of the places you told me you're going, it'd be wise to carry some protection for yourself when you did. Let me know any time if I can help.

THE LITTLE PRINCE

FLOYD T. JACKSON

The pretty, fair-haired receptionist in the Laura Ashley dress smiled. "Oh hi!" she said. "Mr. Jackson said to show you in as soon as you arrived." She came from behind the desk and led the way down the long maroon-carpeted corridor with a line of Redouté rose prints along one wall to a door near the end. The nameplate on it read "Floyd T. Jackson. Deputy Manager: Personnel." She tapped on the door and held it open.

A dapper man with short black hair, in a gray business suit, a white shirt with a button-down collar and a royal blue tie: he had a firm handshake, and his voice was quiet. He pulled two low armchairs to a coffee table by the window.

I'm glad you could make it, good to meet you. An hour you said? And again next Tuesday, and the Tuesday after? That'll suit me fine. The end of the month I go to Cincinnati for a conference so that'll work in just right.

Well, like you said, I haven't prepared anything: we'll go where the conversation takes us, okay? One thing I want to say straight at the beginning though is I had a good childhood. Lots of folk say they didn't don't they? They say a bad childhood was responsible for everything that happened and everything they did. All the fault of their childhood, right? Well I don't, no, not me: I had a real good childhood in every way, I want to make that plain.

My family wasn't rich, not rich at all if we're talking money and material things. As far as those things go we were downright poor. But in all other ways we were rich, you know what I mean? In things that mattered—love, care, concern—I never lacked for those, never for one day in all my childhood life I did not and that's a fact. Four good strong women raised me, every one of them good and every one of them strong: my mother, my grandmother, and two of my aunts. We all of us lived in a nice clean house in a good neighborhood in Detroit: and we always had food and we always had clothes. Not much of anything, but always enough of everything for us to get by.

My mother was working; she was a teacher in high school and that meant she had a regular wage. Her being a teacher meant another thing too: she was a well-educated woman, with lots of certificates and things. My mother had something special about her, you know what I mean? She was a good hardworking person and was always trying to put it into me that when I grew up I should be the same.

The great idol of her life was a man by the name of Booker T. Washington; did you ever hear that name? Yes you're absolutely right, that's who he was: the founder of the very first university for black people in Tuskegee, Alabama, in 1881. And my mother always used to say to me, "Floyd" she'd say, "now you just remember Booker T. Washington, how he showed how important education is to a black man, and you always try as hard as you can to be like him." And I remember other times she'd say to me "Floyd, if you can master just two subjects, English and math, then there'll be nothing in your life you can't deal with no matter what it is, whether it's a work problem or an emotional one. If you know English and math, you'll be equipped for every situation in life you'll ever come across."

A pity I didn't heed her words you know, then when I was young: I've often thought maybe I would have too, if only I'd had me some competition in the family. But the trouble was you see that I didn't: no brothers or sisters, and in a family of four women I was the only male. In fact, I didn't have no male relatives at all: the only others near my own age were two cousins that I had, and they were both female too. So you see what I was as a kid was I was everybody's pet. Everybody loved me because I was special, and what was special about me was I was male. I wasn't exactly spoiled, I wouldn't say that: but from the earliest age I remember I was kind of looked up to because one day I'd be a man, you know what I mean? I was the little prince waiting to come into his kingdom sort of thing, and because of that I was always well behaved: good at school, worked hard, never played hookey, and well thought of by all my teachers, too. Outside of that, I was a member of the church, a Cub Scout, in every way a model boy. I didn't ever do wrong: I couldn't and I wouldn't, I just wasn't that kind.

It stayed that way the whole of the first ten, eleven years of my life. Till my father came back into it, in fact.

But don't think I'm blaming him for things, because I'm not. I don't recall I'd ever seen him before. I suppose I might have, but he and my mother had separated when I was six months old. Maybe now I think of it it could have been they weren't married ever, I'm not sure. I know he went off and lived with another lady and I never saw him until I was old enough to be a person. Up until then any kid he saw in the street could have been his, and he only began to take an interest in me when I was forming some character of my own. That's how it often is with fathers, right?

He was a longshoreman, someone who works on the waterfront loading and unloading vessels, a stevedore I believe it's sometimes called as well. And he started calling around at our house once a week, usually Saturday afternoon. I think my mother hoped maybe he was going to renew his interest in her. He was a very tall man, good-looking, you know? That's often how it is with women isn't it; no matter how badly a guy's treated her she hopes he'll maybe change? Well in his case it wasn't so: he only ever asked could he take me out a couple of hours, to the park or someplace like that. My mother and grandmother said to him "Okay then, but just you see it is the park, and none of them bars of yours." And he'd say "No of course not, what sort of a guy do you think I am? I'd not ever even think of doing that with a kid of his age.'' Then he'd turn so they couldn't see him, and he'd give me a big wink.

Because that'd be exactly where he would take me, every time; round all his favorite bars. I was small for my age, like I'm still small now, and this big man who was my father, he'd lift me up and set me on the bar everywhere we went for everyone to see. He'd call out, ''Hey come on and meet my son everybody. This is Joe junior, ain't he a fine-looking boy?'' My name wasn't ''Joe,'' and I don't think he ever knew what it really was or cared: but his name was Joe, so I was ''Joe junior'' which was all that mattered to him.

After a time it got so they all always kept a special glass for me with ''Joe junior'' on it behind the bar; it was for a soda or something for me every time we went in. And I'll tell you something now: very soon I did, I came to like him very much, that man. Something of a rogue he may have been, sure, but he wasn't no villain and there's a difference you know, there really is. He was big and tall and good-looking, and there was a twinkle in his eye. He had a way with the ladies, and he was my father, and I hoped often enough that when I grew up I'd be like him. He always made me promise never to tell my mother or grandmother where we'd been, and I never did; that would have been the end of our trips out together if ever they'd gotten to know.

Many times I wished he'd come back home and live with my mother and grandmother and me, I really did, and sometimes I told him that. And he'd smile at me and pat me on the head; he'd say ''Boy you know what, that'd be really nice, one day we'll see what we can work out about it, heh?'' I mentioned it to my grandmother one time and I remember her face went all kind of tight. She said ''Floyd, now you don't even think about that ever, do you hear me?'' But I did.

I guess that's enough for me to tell you about my childhood though, right? What went wrong with my life after, that's the question we come to isn't it? Well believe me, if I could tell you a simple answer, I would, but the truth is and always has been I honestly don't know. But suddenly I started playing hookey from school: one day one week, two days the next, and so on like that. And it wasn't I was being bullied there or my lessons fell off or my grades were poor. It was just I was playing around: or certainly it was at the beginning, and that was all.

Parts of Detroit, like in every city I guess, they were known as not very good environments: they were in every way not at all like the part I lived in, so they were where I always went. There were drugs around, liquor, and plenty of girls, and for some reason to me, that suddenly started to feel like where I belonged. I was restless and school was boring; being good was like I'd been missing out, that's the nearest I can get. What mattered was to experience life, so I tried everything there was. My first time of taking drugs, of drinking myself incapable, of having full sex with a girl—they all happened with a rush, just within a few weeks of me being fourteen. All the guys I mixed with there were around that same age, and nothing was important to all of us except to do everything, and as much of all of it as we could.

I look back at it now you know, and I think it was all somehow weird: weird is the only word I can possibly use. There were maybe two hundred kids around there and all of them behaving that selfsame way. No one did anything terrible, don't get me wrong: there weren't no guns or knives and fights or stuff like that. Maybe a bit of petty crime, burglarizing houses for small change, shoplifting, stealing from our parents, taking small items from our homes. That was how we all lived and we all thought it was happiness. And the biggest buzz of all was in having our own society which was just the other side of the law. It went on that way I guess about three years.

Maybe it's not too unusual for kids, I mean to go through a phase like that: maybe it's something most of them do for a while and then grow out of. I was never in serious trouble though, none of us were. But the police learned most of our names, and they had our number: we had the potential for one day getting into serious crime. They began coming around our homes now and again and asking us a few questions. We'd not done anything, but I guess they were giving a hint to our parents it was time they should be watching out for us, you know how I mean?

And if that was what it was, it worked for sure for my mother. Once she'd gotten over the shock of finding I was no longer her precious little boy devoting his time to education in the way she understood it, and which naturally caused her a great deal of distress and worry, she sat me down for a serious talk. She asked me to tell her straight just exactly what was wrong with the way she'd been raising me. Well, I could no more tell her then than I've been able to tell you now. All I could say was it wasn't I was unhappy, but I felt I wanted to broaden my knowledge of life, that was all. She asked me did I want to squander the hard work I'd already put in on my education, or did I want to go on trying to make something good for myself in my future. I told her yes I did: so she said she'd think about it a while very carefully and talk with my grandmother and my aunts about it. Then we'd all discuss it all together and see what we could come up with in the way of ideas.

What they finally said was this: they said they thought the real trouble was I needed to learn how to discipline myself, not rely on other folks like her and school to do it for me. And she thought maybe a spell in the armed forces would help me learn how. It was a good life, a man's life, it paid good, there was opportunities for travel and new experiences, and I'd not be leading such a sheltered life like I had so far, in a household that was entirely female like ours. Well, that appealed to me, I thought it made sense, so it didn't take much effort on her part to persuade me that the sooner I started in on it, the better it would be.

I've an appointment at four, so should we maybe finish at that point for today and pick it up again from there next week? Sure, same day same time, that'd suit me fine.

Where'd we finish last time? Oh sure, when I joined the navy at seventeen, I remember, that's right. Well, I signed on for four years, and I did, I really enjoyed the life. To a boy from a Detroit suburb, it was a great adventure you know, I went all over the world: Germany, Norway, Denmark, the Philippines, I even once briefly visited your country, England. We put into a place called Portsmouth I think it

was, on the south coast there. A really cute little town I remember it
as: very quaint, old-fashioned streets and houses and things. From
there we had a couple of days seeing London as well: Buckingham
Palace, Windsor Palace where your queen lives, and somewhere else
there was an old old cathedral called Salsboro or some name like that,
would that be it?

I liked the navy, always all the time seeing those new places: and I
learned some new skills in it too. I was a maintenance engineer: and
before long I was promoted to be a petty officer and had maybe
around twenty men under me, so I guess I was doing pretty good. I
didn't see it that way, but I should have signed on for twenty years.
And maybe I wouldn't have ended where I did if I had you know. I
often think that: I was my own man, I earned good money, I had
responsibility, and I could have made a good life for myself, I could.
But I didn't; instead I hooked up with guys who were doing bad
things, just like I'd done when I was home. I was drinking and gambling and whoring whenever we were in a port, and there were four of
us in particular who formed our own little team. Every place we went,
as soon as we got ashore it was where's the action, where's the bars,
where are the girls? Dissolution, that was our life. Before, it'd been
with kids, but now it was with grown men. Two of us were eighteen
and two of us were twenty-one, and if you saw one of us around, the
others'd always be somewhere near, you could rely on that. And because of it, what happened happened: one for all and all for one. I
don't want to say the responsibility for the final outcome was anyone
else's though, it wouldn't be true: the main fault was mine.

And this is the way it came about, just around the time the four
years I'd signed on for were coming to their end. We put into port on
the East Coast, and we had a ten-day furlough, our final one, and even
by our own low standards, what we raised was hell. We had competi-
tions every day: which one of us could drink the most liquor and stay
standing, which one could win the largest bet at roulette, who could
screw the most girls one after another in twenty-four hours. We went
on that way for eight days I guess, maybe nine, and then finally one

night we all got ourselves involved in a big fight in a downtown bar. Usually I let the others do the serious fighting because I was the smallest, but this particular night there was no chance of that, there were fists flying everywhere. Everyone fought: furniture was smashed, bottles and glasses broken, everything. And I saw one of my buddies was backed up in a corner, with three guys standing in a bunch with their fists raised, ready to give him a beating.

Like I said, all for one and one for all. I didn't stop to think about it, I went behind them, and I gave one an almighty punch, just as hard as I could. Where I caught him was here in the side of his throat, and he dropped to the floor like he was a bag of potatoes. I'd fractured a vein or burst a blood vessel, I've never known exactly what, but whatever, right there and then he was instantly dead. I didn't know it, I thought he was just unconscious or something, but me and my buddy didn't stay to find out. And I felt quite proud of myself for what I'd done.

We went back to the ship real quick: we thought it was the safest place to be. What we didn't expect though was who came to see us the next day: it was the police. They asked us to go with them and answer a few questions about the fight there'd been in this bar: a guy in it had been killed. Was I the one who'd done it? Half a dozen people who were there were going to say they'd seen me deliver that blow.

It does something to you, something like that. It's like nothing you've ever experienced in your life. A guy who was a living person, another human being: now he's no more, and it's due only to you. Your lives are inextricable, but you're alive and he's dead, and you caused that and it can never be undone. Something went out of me at that moment in my life; and now all of these years later, it's never come back and it never will. I got a life sentence for murder, and I think I was lucky I didn't go to the chair, it was only that that state didn't have the death penalty then, that was all.

Prison's the only place in the world you can go where there's nothing else for you to do but think, and it took me the whole of the first seven years in there before I got my thinking straight, it really did.

I wasn't going to let myself admit I'd really killed a guy, you know what I mean? I was all the time making excuses about it: it'd been an accident because I hadn't meant to do it; or he'd had a weak carotid artery; or he'd seen the punch coming and tried to duck out of it but he'd miscalculated and ducked into it instead. And anyway what if I hadn't hit him? Him and those guys with him, they'd have beaten my buddy to death. So what, if I had killed one man I'd saved the life of another. On and on I went, every variation I could think of, trying to think of an escape. Like I say, for seven years I did that, but finally I stopped. I don't know why. Perhaps because I ran out of excuses, that's all, but in the end I recognized them for what they were and accepted the fault was no one else's but mine.

The person who helped me most was my mother. In spite of what I'd done, she never gave up on me. Every single month she made a five-hundred-mile round trip to the prison to visit me. She came on the Greyhound bus when she'd finished school Friday afternoon, traveled all night and came to see me Saturday, stopped over in a nearby cheap motel, then Sunday took the bus again back home. She wrote me once every week, and what she wrote or said when she came to see me was always the same. She said "Son, there's still good in you like there is in everyone. You done wrong, and the one person who can help you do right again is you." She never blamed me, she never told me stop trying to find excuses for myself, she just said on and on she loved me and she wanted me to start over my life again when the day came that I came out. She said "Take this chance you've got now to go on improving your education." So I did: I worked in the prison print shop, and all the time I could spare I read and I read. I took a business administration course and got my diploma for it; it wasn't something much, but it was a start for a new way of thinking for me, you know what I mean?

With my mother's help and all the books and magazines I read that she was always sending in to me, I got very slowly to see I was young enough to make something of myself still. I did seventeen years: when I went in I was twenty-three years of age and when I came out I was just on forty-one. And all I can say of it is this, that when I went in I was stupid and irresponsible, and when I came out half my lifetime later, at last I was a mature and thoughtful man. Five years ago that was now: let's talk about how it went from there next time shall we, if that's okay?

Some folks might say I was institutionalized by prison. In a lot of ways I'd have to agree with them—it's correct, I was. On my record it'd show I was nearly a model prisoner: for the full seventeen years I was quiet and well behaved, and never got written up for an infraction of prison rules, not once in all that time. A thing that helped was I never wore a watch. It's harder to live under the prison system if you're thinking all the time When'll I get out, when'll I be free? But I taught myself not to think that way. I'd done wrong, I'd done a bad thing; the world didn't owe me a living, it was me that owed one to the world. Doing time was the only thing I could do to pay: not adequately, not even approximately, but it was the only way. When I'd done enough, society would say so, not me. There wasn't no point in me getting frustrated, I'd just forget the subject was there.

When they told me six months ahead I was going to go out, right off I started to write letters to anyone I could think of that might give me a job. I didn't have any personal friends or contacts, but my mother provided me with some business directories, and I scoured them for any sort of firm I thought might give me a chance. I wrote them who I was and where, and exactly why I'd been in prison for seventeen years. I didn't have much to offer in qualifications except for my business studies diploma, but I said I'd start at the bottom and if they'd give me a probationary period, meantime before I came out I'd read up everything I could find if they'd tell me what their special subjects and interests were.

You know what? The response I got was amazing: I'd never have believed how many people there were who if you were straight with them, they'd consider giving you a chance. All this stuff you read in newspapers about people not wanting to know if you're a transgressor, it just wasn't true. I guess I had something like twenty-five replies: the majority said they were sorry they didn't have anything, but wished me luck and they'd keep my name on file. But six in total, they were really positive, they told me to come see them when I got out. That was such a lift to my spirits you know, I can't describe.

And that's how it went. I started with a small concern that made auto engine parts—in their offices, kind of a general clerk. I stopped there six months, then one day one of their customers asked me if I'd go work for him. I was real nervous, I mean about telling him my record, because he didn't know it, did he? So before I accepted I gave him the full story, and said if he wanted to withdraw the offer I'd have no hard feelings. But he said no, I'd been honest with him and he thanked me for it. And his offer still held.

You know all of it was truly amazing, and it set me to thinking if so many people were doing what they were, taking a risk and giving me a chance, then the least I could do was go on seriously trying to improve myself even more and build up my confidence. So I enrolled myself in night school and went to classes two evenings a week: I studied beginners' psychology and personnel management work.

For a year, I lived very simply. I had a one-room apartment, I kept away from any kind of trouble, I didn't drink, not even a drop; I saved a little money and I went on and on studying every second of my time. Then I got a really big break: I got taken on by this big company I'm with now, whose name is known very widely in the Midwest and everywhere. I read of the vacancy in a newspaper and told them my record. And with it I had recommendations about my character from the two companies I'd worked for, plus a statement on my progress from the college where I was studying. And they were people yet again who gave me a chance. I had to take a cut in salary to start with them, but to have the opportunity to work for a concern this size is what matters: if you want it, you've a job the rest of your life.

It was two years ago I came here, and in the time since I've worked hard and I've continued my studies. What I am now is deputy personnel manager for this whole area: and even if I say it myself, I think that's pretty good compared with where I was five years ago. Life looks good, and I've had one other big break that I don't deserve, the best a man can have: I've married a lovely lady, and we have our own apartment too, in a good part of town. She and my mother who lives with us now, they get along together just fine, and in three months' time if nothing goes wrong, we shall then have our first child. "Life begins at forty" right? You know what I mean?

EVERYTHING'S POSSIBLE
WITH GOD

REV. CURTIS COOPER

*O*n Saturday morning by ten o'clock the temperature was already almost one hundred degrees. His house was a freshly painted blue-and-white bungalow, one of a line of trim homes set along an avenue of well-tended lawns. Slim, handsome and long legged, he had the build of an athlete: he wore an open-necked tartan shirt and newly pressed stone-washed blue jeans. Beyond the sitting room in the dining alcove a three-year-old in red cotton shorts pedaled round and round the table on his yellow plastic tricycle humming determinedly.

Lionel, don't go so fast now, you'll make yourself dizzy and fall off. Go in the kitchen and ride there instead, okay? Good morning brother it's a pleasure to meet you, please sit yourself down. Lionel fetch some juice from the icebox for this gentleman will you please? Yes you can have another one if you want one and I will too, bring me one as well. Are you cool enough there brother? Move nearer the air conditioner or is it making too much noise? Excuse me? Sure, we could switch it off altogether if you want, it'll be mighty hot though if we do: we'll have it off a while then take a break and then switch it back on again okay? Heh Lionel, what are you doing out there? Yeah you can have some cookies, only hurry up with that juice now will you there's a good man.

Well brother you've come a long way to see me, I hope you'll think it worthwhile. Did you see my church on the corner as you came by? I'm the assistant pastor there, yeah that's the very one that's mine.

Did you see the red brick building at the side of it there? We opened it just last year and my wife works there, she's one of our secretaries. That's what's called the Harmony Center where the administration office is. Thanks Lionel, careful now, put the gentleman's juice on that table for him. Be good and quiet now like you promised won't you so's him and me can have a little talk? Say why not go and play with Jo-Jo and Louise in their house, mm? Oh yes you do like girls too you do, don't give me that. Well if you stay here you must make no noise: remember your promise Lionel? Yes, I just said that, you go and play with Jo-Jo and Louise. Good-bye now, good-bye, I'll come for you there.

Peace at last brother, okay now where'll I start? Who am I? Well I'm the Reverend Curtis Cooper and I'm assistant pastor of that little church. It has a congregation of about one hundred and fifty souls and I was appointed there when I came out of prison which is two years ago in June. I had a sentence of twenty years to life which I got for murder when I was sixteen: if I'd been any older I'd have got the electric chair. I saw it as just my age but later I came to realize it was more: it was a sign of God's plan for me, that he'd chosen me to live and carry out his will. It was a long journey I had to take though before it came clear.

I was born in Montgomery the state capital of Alabama, as you're probably aware. My father I never knew: he worked on the railroad and was killed in an accident there just two weeks before my birth. One day he went off in the morning and he never came back; my mother didn't know what had happened until a messenger was sent to tell her the following day. Things like that happen with black workers, no one thinks they're important you see. I've seen pictures of my father and he looked like someone I'd like to have known. I'd been his only child. Then my mother married again and with my stepfather she had four girls. My stepfather was a good hardworking man and he treated me no different from them but then he got a sickness and he died as well. That meant my mother had five children to raise all on her own.

She used to tell me I'd been good at school: I know I got good grades. I'd like to have gone on to high school and college maybe, but that was only a dream: we were a poor family and me being a boy and the eldest one, I had to help at home half of my time. Mother worked hard: she was a cook at one school and a cleaner at another. I stayed home in her place and took care of my sisters: I kept house, gave them their meals, took them to school and brought them back again. I was thirteen that's all, so I didn't have proper schooling. And I never had a proper childhood of my own either. I couldn't go out and hang around, I was kind of an oddball and didn't have friends. I don't recall I was too unhappy about it though, I couldn't say that; when you're a kid you take life as it comes. Besides, when I got older it gave me an excuse to tell people about my childhood neglect. I told them all the things I hadn't had: I told myself that too, I made it the reason for what I was doing, which was breaking into people's homes and stealing from them.

Soon I was leading a double life, you know, like that guy in the story called Dr. Jekyll and the dark side of him whose name was Mr. Hyde. I was a good boy at school who tried to keep up and read books and worked hard at his lessons, and he looked after his sisters too when he was at home. But the other part of me no one knew about. My mother suspected it was there but she didn't know how to deal with it. Some evenings I'd go over the other side of town and drink in bars and play pool, and some nights I didn't go home till maybe two and three o'clock in the morning. My mother was waiting up worrying for me and wondering what kind of trouble I was in because I'd had radios and jewelry she knew I couldn't afford, but she'd be scared of asking me where I'd got them and she didn't want to know the truth which was I'd stolen them out of people's homes.

I don't want to speak badly of my mother: she was weak, she was lonely and twice she'd had husbands who died and left her on her own. She had a family mental weakness too: when I was fifteen she had a nervous breakdown. She had to go into a hospital for that electric shock treatment and was there nearly a year. My aunt who was her sister came to live in our house with her husband to look after me and two of my sisters: the other two went to another aunt up in Baltimore. That broke the family up and it never recovered: it was all a sad time for everyone.

After that I don't think I went to school hardly ever again. I said I did, I left first thing in the morning saying I was going there: afternoons I'd come home again at the right time. But I wasn't spending my time in academic studies, I was educating myself in a different way. I stole a lot, I took automobiles and went joy-riding, I smoked dope, I had girls. I was a hustler entirely, and nothing more. And you'll always find like-minded people of your own age if you're that sort: there's a subculture of young people, and that's what I joined. All my time I spent enjoying myself with others like me, and if you'd seen us you'd have thought none of us had a care in the world. I know I hadn't: I didn't see what that life would lead me into, and if anyone'd tried to tell me I wouldn't have listened.

I was tall, I was strong, and though I say it myself I was good-looking too. In near every group I was in, even if most of the others in it were older than me, I was always the one took the lead. I don't know why it should have been but usually people deferred to me. If I said we should do something everyone else agreed and was ready to go along. I'd work out burglaries for us and pick who was to do them with me and be a member of my team. Mostly we only ever took money: not things like valuables because they could be identified. A couple of times it meant putting a gun to someone's head and telling them to keep quiet. We weren't bank robbers, we broke into houses and a few times held up shopkeepers in small corner stores: I thought I was real brave and one hell of a guy. To me I was headed for the big time and a real life of crime and I was only fifteen. After a while I told my aunt and uncle I'd had a job as a salesman offered me in a store the other side of town, so I was leaving home to take some of the financial burden off them and going to live with a friend. Part of it was true, but I didn't reveal to them the friend was a girl, and I didn't say the job wasn't selling things in stores but taking things from them instead.

I guess now's the time for telling you what I was put away on my life sentence for, and brother I don't find this easy to talk about but you've come to see me because I said that I would. Because it says in the Bible we should do that which is honest though we be as reprobates, for we can do nothing against the truth. So that's what I'll do. I'll not try to excuse it either: I played the most part in it, and from the beginning it was all my idea.

I'd heard through a man there was an old lady and she kept money in her house where she lived, a place in a residential area on the south edge of town. She was there on her own except she had a guard dog for protection, a big bull mastiff or something of that sort. But this creature had recently died and she hadn't yet taken another one in its place but was having one the following week. That meant for a few days going there robbing her, it would be safe. I talked it over with a couple of other guys and the girl that I lived with, and it looked like it would be a pushover if we didn't delay. The plan was to steal an automobile and drive out there: the old lady wouldn't open her door to three strangers but she might if she thought it was just a girl on her own. We'd stay out of sight while she told her some tale about being lost and needing help and asking to use the telephone, and when the old lady let her in we'd be right there behind her and get inside. We went a couple of days earlier to look at the place and it looked pretty good: there was no other house near it and its front was hidden by bushes from the road.

The old lady was eighty years old, and she'd lived all that time without learning there were so many bad people around who looked like you could trust them. Straight away she opened her door when our girl rang the bell; when the other three of us appeared behind her she was so shocked she opened her mouth but couldn't get out a sound. What we told her was true: so long as she kept quiet and did what we said we'd do her no harm, and she just stood there looking helpless with her arms by her sides. We asked her where she kept money and she didn't argue, she took us to the lounge off one side of the hallway and nodded her head at a big old-fashioned sideboard there that had antique plates on it and drawers underneath. I had a gun. It wasn't loaded but she wasn't to know that, and I pointed it at her and told her to back off and stand near the window while one of the others searched the drawers. One of them opened one a little and then it kind of stuck: when he jerked at it to get it loose, one of the plates fell down from off a shelf and smashed in pieces on the floor.

A strange thing about noise is one thing leads to another, noise has a very frightening sound all on its own. Till then the old lady'd been silent and not said a word: but it seemed like the sound of the plate breaking set her off and as soon as it happened she started to yell. For a minute we thought there might be other people in the house we hadn't known about she was shouting to for help, but no one came. She still went on screaming and hollering though and the others all began looking at me waiting for me to tell them what to do. I didn't want to hit her because she was old: I told the girl to take one of the curtain cords and tie her in a chair and use a silk scarf she was wearing as a gag round her mouth. She struggled and screamed though till I made like I was going to hit her on the head: that frightened her a while and then she kept quiet.

The others couldn't find any cash in the drawers of the sideboard, and we all started getting cranky and cross. The old lady kept nodding her head at me, and then she said "Key" through the scarf. She went on saying it until I knew what she meant: there was a key they should get from the drawer; there wasn't money in there, they were wasting their time. When they found it she nodded her head again at a picture on the wall: behind it was her safe.

They opened it and there was maybe a couple of thousand dollars in notes in it, that's all, but for the kind of small-time criminals we were, that was a real big haul. Then the old lady found her voice again: the scarf the girl had tied round her mouth had fallen loose and she was in full voice again and yelling for the police. One of the guys was wearing a cotton sash round his waist, so I made him give it to the girl to put round the old lady's face to keep her quiet. It didn't work; all it did was cover her eyes so she couldn't see us, but every minute her voice got louder like she knew we were scared. I was angry too that she wouldn't keep quiet. I'd not been in that kind of situation before so I panicked.

On a couch by the window was a big cushion. It had a thick red brocade cover on it that was loose: I took it off and pulled it down hard all around the old lady's head. One end of the curtain cord she was tied to the chair with was hanging down and I wound that round her neck to keep the cover in place. Then all of us ran out to the car and left the place quick.

We could hear her shouting as we went so she wasn't killed then. But nobody came to her rescue. By the time they did, I don't know how long it was but when they found her the cushion cover had suffocated her and she was dead. So the old lady died, brother, yeah that old lady died. . . . I have to apologize, I need a few minutes' time. I'll go get me some juice from the kitchen. You want some more too?

Well okay then, yeah. . . .

Next day it was on the TV news and radio everywhere that the old lady'd been murdered: there was appeals to anyone with information about it to come forward and help the police. They said it was a gang had been responsible, three men and a girl, which meant we'd been seen. They didn't have names or descriptions but we were dangerous they said, and people shouldn't approach us because we were most likely armed. They build these things up for the public and make it sound worse than it was: we weren't nothing much else really but very very scared. When they heard it was murder the two other guys just disappeared, and I don't think they were ever caught. That left only me and the girl, and it didn't take long for us to work out if someone called the police and informed on us, that'd be the end. We moved out from our apartment and spent three days and nights in three different motels.

The girl was crying all the time and I was nearly doing the same. We were a couple of kids and each day every minute we were more and more scared. We both of us knew in the end we'd be captured and it'd only go worse for us if we waited for that: the only solution was to give ourselves up and take what was coming to us and be punished like we deserved. It seemed once we'd decided it it was like a big weight had been lifted from our backs. So that's what we did.

When the case came to court, we were sorry and we hadn't meant to kill the old lady was about all we could say. I spoke for the girl and said it was no way her fault, she'd done what I told her to. Maybe that helped her a little because she was treated with leniency: she was given life but did only seven years and then was given parole or at least so I heard. I don't exactly know because we didn't keep contact between us, but I believe she went to Baton Rouge. Like I said because I was sixteen I got a life sentence, not the chair: I was thankful for that because the way I saw it, the death sentence was what I truly deserved.

I was afraid of going into prison, and brother I was right to be. I'd heard bad stories about what happened in those places while I was in custody waiting for my trial; it didn't take long for me to find out they were all true and worse. I'd only been inside a very short time, a matter of weeks that's all, and then the propositions came. If you're a boy when you go inside and a nice-looking one, they can't wait to get you in their hands: you're simply a nice piece of new pussy and that's all. There's only two sorts of approach: one's the guy who comes to you and says, "So long as you stay with me, kid, I'll protect you and you'll be okay. Keep yourself fresh and clean, stay just for me and I'll see you come to no harm." The other kind's the terrorizer: he's tough and doing a long time, and he says to you "Listen now kid and listen good. I'm the one who runs this place and I'm giving you a choice and that's real nice of me because I usually don't give choices, not to anyone at all. It's either you let me have you whenever I feel like it, or you don't and I have you just the same. And the second will bring you pain."

I didn't like any of it and I was terrified, so I put an application in to see the warden straight away. I didn't get to see him though, I saw his deputy instead. When they brought me to his office I asked if his secretary could please go out, because I didn't want to say what I wanted in front of her. When she did step out with a grin on her face he didn't even give me a chance. What he said was "I know what you've come for kid, to ask for protection from sexual harassment. Well save your breath. Every young kid like you who comes in for the first time tells us it, we've heard it all before. There's nothing we can do, and I don't know we would if we could either, do I make myself clear? You've been convicted of killing an old lady right? To my way of thinking you deserved the chair. Now get your ass out of my office and don't bother me no more."

Well, there are bad men in prison and evil men too, and there are men in prison who aren't so bad, even if what they've done is evil in the eyes of the world. Maybe it is. But when they get in there somehow sometimes what's good in them comes out, and they try if they can to help others on their way. It was my good fortune only a couple of days after that incident with the deputy warden to meet one such man, and he told me what to do. He was sitting on his own at a table in the prison dining hall where he worked, and he beckoned me over and told me to meet him outside in the recreation compound in an hour.

I thought he was going to be another one the same as the rest, propositioning; but it wasn't that at all. He was an elderly guy and white, and he told me he'd been incarcerated nearly all his life: he never expected to be free because long ago he'd murdered and violated a child. He knew most of everything that went on in the prison he said, and from the talk he'd heard he knew three guys at least were after me. He knew who they were and what they were, and they weren't as tough as they liked to make out. They were betting each other which one would get to me the first. He looked me in the eye and he said "Do you mind that idea son, do you want to be somebody's fuck-boy?" I said no I did not, most definitely no, so he said "Well here's what you should do about it then. Tonight at six o'clock when everyone's watching the ball game on TV, go down the corridor where the classrooms are and to the ablutions section on the right at the end. There's two old toilets in there," he said, "which no one uses much now. Climb up on the seat of the one on the left and put your hand up in the cistern of it and feel around. You'll find a knife in there, at the bottom of it under the water. Take it out and hide it on you, tuck it in your sock on your leg down here. Then come out and walk around a while: when you see one of the guys who've been hassling you, give him a nod. Let him follow you some place where you can face him. Then take out the knife and stick it towards him, and say three words to him, that's all. Say them through your teeth too so's he'll know you mean them: say 'Leave me alone.' Do that to each of them, then go to the toilet and put back the knife in the water and I'll collect it from there."

And he went on some more: he told me what prison was about. Most of all it was reputation he said; once you had one it would last you as long as you were there. When I made it plain I wasn't the sort to be messed with, no one would try it with me again. Well, he was perfectly right: after I'd done it just exactly the way he said, no one ever tried. Not the guys who'd hassled me nor anyone else, not in the whole of the rest of my sentence.

For a long time it was hard. I had the thought many times during my incarceration that I'd never be free, and unlike a lot of the guys whose families stood by them, unfortunately mine never did. Soon after my trial my mother died, and from my sisters I never again heard a word. Me killing an old lady by strangling and suffocating her was something they couldn't forgive. None of them wrote or came to see me, not ever, and when I wrote to them, they never replied, they gave me no chance to explain. But God did, God forgave me I'm sure. And the reason I know that is what I'll tell you now brother, and with gladness in my heart.

It was after I'd been in prison seven or eight years that I first went to church, which was something I hadn't ever done before in the whole of my life. Once a month a group called the First Church of God's Holy Word came in on a Saturday and had a service in the chapel, and any person who wanted to was free to go along. Some of them were young people who brought guitars: they followed the text in Ephesians which tells you "Speak to yourselves in psalms and hymns and spiritual songs, singing and making melody in your heart to the Lord." And they had a special kind of joy about them, it very much appealed to me because being happy's not a feeling comes to you often when you're in prison. Yet when I went there to the meetings those people held, for an hour or two I'd forget my sadness and feel a lift in my soul.

They were popular with a lot of the guys, so then they were given permission to extend the number of times they came. They started Bible classes, then meetings for witness, and more and more I began to see that what Jesus had said was true: "I am the door, and by me if any man enter in, he shall be saved." There was one young lady I specially liked talking to. Her name was Theodora which means "gifts of God" and you could see in her face she had inner happiness, and she witnessed to me. She gave me a Bible and marked out passages in it for me to read, following the precept that Isaiah speaks of, that "the deaf shall hear the words of the book, and the eyes of the blind shall see."

Then came a special day: she said she'd prayed about me to God and He'd told her to tell me to go along a special way, to enroll in her church's correspondence course in theology, for an eventual purpose which would later be revealed. I couldn't think what that could be for a man sentenced to spend the rest of his natural life in prison, but I was happy to do it without knowing the outcome, since she was my guide. Jesus said that "for men some things were impossible but with God all things are possible," so with this young lady's faith to support me I was content, and I applied myself to the necessary studies without expectations concerning the future of any kind.

Over the three years that followed I devoted myself with her help to studying God's word until I had every one of my certificates and I reached the standard necessary for being ordained. I made enquiries to the state prison authorities to see if that would be possible, and how it came about I don't know, but somehow it was conveyed to me that it could coincide later with a release on parole. And that was what came to pass: the church here offered work for me and accommodation as well, and two years ago I came here and have been here ever since with my wife and my stepson Lionel, the boy you've already seen. God has showered His blessings on me in every way, because as the Bible tells us "Ye shall know the truth, and the truth shall set you free."

How it came about that I met and married my wife was another example of it too. She came to visit a prisoner with another lady who was his wife and a friend of hers, and I passed through the visiting room when they were in it, to put some more stock in the Coke-dispensing machine. I knew this man slightly, and he knew I had no visitors ever came to see me, so he called me over and I stopped by their table a while and we talked. A week after that I had a letter from her saying she'd enjoyed visiting with me and asking would I like her to write, to which I replied I'd like that very much indeed. From there on in, a correspondence developed between us, and before long she took to coming to see me once a month or so on her own. We became good friends because she was a person who also had been saved, and then she brought young Lionel to meet me because he had no daddy of his own. So even though I was in prison the three of us developed a great bond. When I was told what release date I'd been given I asked her straight away would she marry me when I came out. When she said yes she would, we fixed it for the day after that, which was now two years ago. I never thought I'd find such happiness ever in my life you know brother, truly I never did. My wife, my work, our little boy, our home: the freedom to breathe and to see the sky and smell the flowers that bloom in the spring.

I told you my wife worked in the Harmony Center there, right? That's where she is this morning, but at midday she'll be coming home. She's a shy person and reserved with strangers, but I asked her would she talk with you, and after some hesitation at first she agreed. When she arrives I'm going to collect Lionel like always and take him to the park. She and you'll get along fine and you'll find her interesting to talk to too: she's been in prison and done time for killing someone, just like me.

II

WOMEN OF THE WORLD

THREE RELEASED WOMEN

IT'S A HELP SOMETIMES, YES AND NO

DORIS COOPER

Did Curtis tell you talking's something I don't do a lot of? I only said I would to please him. I don't want to be rude or anything, but I don't have long. There's something I've got to go back and finish at the center. We're very busy right now.

High cheekboned, tall and black with deep brown eyes: wearing jeans and a white sweatshirt, she sat barefooted on the settee with her legs pulled up, resting her chin on her knees and rubbing them gently with it while she talked. Her voice was tight and clipped, her sentences staccato at first until she felt more at ease.

With most people I don't tell them at first I've been in prison, I like to weigh them up before I do. You never know how they're going to react, especially men. You've been in prison, you're a woman. The two things seem hard to fit together for them.

I graduated from high school but I wasn't a scholar. All I was interested in in life was sport. I liked volleyball best. I was good at it, I made the school team. I was quick and I had height. It never bothered me throwing myself around. I was very competitive. I still am, I'm thirty-two and I still like to win when I play games with Curtis and Lionel. I've never been a girly sort of girl. I don't go in for makeup and perfume and that stuff. Sometimes I think I was meant to have been a boy.

My mother and father were from a good educational background.

We had a decent home. I'm the youngest of four girls. My father was in a bank. I loved him a lot. When I was around twelve or thirteen he used to tell me I was his special favorite. When I was that age I was. This is difficult, I mean the subject. It's caused me a lot of confusion when I think about it. I loved him but I didn't like him because of what I've been talking about. What? Okay then yeah, what I haven't been talking about, I guess I'll try and get it said. It's a common story. I didn't know that though at the time, I thought I was the only person it had happened to in the world. When I went in prison I was twenty-two and I still thought it. It was only when I heard other women talking so often about it that I realized how much it went on. It wasn't unusual at all. It seemed like those that hadn't been sexually abused when they were young by their fathers were the minority. It was a long time before I could talk about it, even there: I wouldn't open up and tell anyone it happened to me as well. It's still difficult for me so I'd rather not go into detail about it. But it did leave me with a feeling of bitterness. It seemed like he'd betrayed me, it's hard to explain exactly. Someone who I loved and admired was doing things to me which I felt he shouldn't be doing. I was ashamed at letting him do them, and I knew they must be wrong because he made me promise not to tell anyone. It was only last year I found he'd been doing it with one of my sisters too, and that's made me even more confused.

The biggest effect it had on me is it made me want to leave home as soon as I could. When I went to college after graduating from high school it was my intention to take science subjects there and then follow on from that by joining the military. Only while I was at college I fell in love with another student, a guy my own age, and we started living together. It's difficult for me to separate what my genuine feelings for him were with the idea that I'd been somehow abnormal, because of what I'd done with my father. I think I had the idea somehow things would straighten themselves out if I was into a proper boy-girl relationship. And so I got pregnant by this guy and then he said we should do the right thing and get married. His name was Chuck.

Well I guess anyone would have known the marriage wouldn't work, and it didn't, straight from the start. We quarreled most every day and then one time he slapped me in my face. I told him I wasn't going to take that, if he ever did it again I'd leave him and go home to my mother. By that time she'd been left by my father and she always said she'd like it if we lived together. Two days after, Chuck and I had another quarrel and he hit me once more, so I did what I'd told him I would, I went home. The next day he came there almost crying, he said he was sorry and please would I go back with him. Against my better judgment, and against my mother's advice as well, I decided to give it another go. Then again within a day or two he hit me some more but this time really hard. So it was home to mother again, and again he came and apologized and asked for me to give him another chance.

It's easy to look back and see now that I must have been completely crazy in agreeing, because it went on the same way: I think maybe four or five times I left him then went back again. It was because I was very mixed up: I wanted to love him and for us to have a baby, and I thought if we did in the end it would all work out. But each time we quarreled he hit me harder and harder and I got to be more and more frightened of him. I fought with my mother because I wouldn't keep my word and make a final break, even though all the quarrels he and I had were about stupid silly things. It was like he couldn't live with me because I was all the time irritating him, but he couldn't live without me either.

What happened in the end was I was sitting at the table one night when he came in, I was preparing a meal, cutting up some steak with a long knife. I was seven months pregnant and I was having a hard time, a lot of pain in my legs and always feeling very weary. We began having an argument again and he started shouting and pulling my hair. I had no idea what I was doing; he was pulling me backwards and I stood up still holding the knife and stabbed him. Only once and in the throat and he was dead in a few seconds because I hit the jugular vein. The blood just absolutely gushed out of him.

I went to the hallway where there was a phone and called up the police. I gave my name and address and I said they should come there at once, I'd just killed someone. I said "someone," I didn't say he was my husband or say his name, I don't know why.

I was charged with homicide. I pleaded guilty and drew a sentence of twenty years to life. Right after the hearing I had a miscarriage and I lost my baby. I felt there was nothing for me to go on living for. I've read it's not all that unusual for women in that kind of a situation to try and kill themselves. I don't know why I didn't, I think I felt too numb to even bother to try.

In prison I was put to work in the kitchen. For the whole of the first year I was there I never spoke to anyone, not to anyone at all except to bad-mouth them if they gave me any annoyance for anything, even if it was trivial and unimportant. Because I'm tall and look strong people were sometimes scared of me, especially because I had a bad temper. So I never had hassle, but I didn't make any friends. I did have one experience though which had a lot of effect on me: I was in prison with four hundred women, and it was the first time I'd ever come across lesbianism. Up till then I hadn't even known what it was, and it opened my eyes. After the experiences I'd been through with my father and then with Chuck, I'd developed a strong hatred for men, so why I didn't become a lesbian myself I've no idea. I didn't but what I did have though was the opportunity to learn about feminism and homosexuality and be tolerant towards them: I could see how important they were in some women's lives. I'm not a woman homosexual and I'm not a one hundred percent feminist, but I'm not so ignorant now about those subjects like I was before.

Because mine was a first offense and I'd no record of other felonies or even misdemeanors, according to the law of the state where I was I became eligible to apply for parole after I'd done a third of my sentence. I was given it first time, I got my parole just a little after seven years. The main thing of it was that I came out, but I'm still under some restrictions. I can't vote, and I can't move from one place to somewhere else to live without notifying the authorities and getting permission. Another condition is I'm not supposed to hang around with known felons; that's a laugh isn't it, with me being married to one?

I think being incarcerated was a very bad experience: when I came out I didn't have a friend anywhere in the world. My mother had remarried and I lived with her and her husband but we didn't get on, and I didn't lead any kind of a settled life at all. I worked a while as a waitress, then in a mail-order warehouse, and then as a domestic in a hospital and some other things. Several jobs I tried for but didn't get because you always have to state on your application form whether you've any convictions for felony or not, and if you don't tell the truth you can find yourself in big trouble. But people won't admit it to you if they don't take you on that it's because you've told them the truth. They discriminate against you and don't say the reason why, they say there's someone else with better qualifications than you. That doesn't sound all that convincing when what you're applying for is a job in a hotel kitchen cleaning out garbage bins.

I was very vulnerable and during this time I was involved very briefly in a relationship with a man who gave me a job. He had a wife already, and I knew that but I was desperate for some affection from anyone. We made love properly I think it was only a total of three times. As soon as he found I'd become pregnant he fired me, and I was as low then as I've ever been. I wanted very much though to have something or someone in life who was mine, so I decided however difficult it was going to be I'd go ahead and have the baby, and he was Lionel. His father's never given me a cent in maintenance costs and I've never seen him from that day on.

My mother was good about it and I don't know how I'd have made out if it hadn't been for her. There was a neighbor too who was kind and helpful to me a lot and sometimes I'd go and visit with her and tell her my troubles. She had little kids of her own and she was a widow, so she knew what it was like to be having a hard time. One day she told me she had a present for me, she'd been specially and bought it in the mall. It was a Bible, and she said whenever I felt sad or lonely,

I should open it just at any page at all, I'd always find something written there that would give me comfort. Since that day I've always read my Bible every day without fail and it was true what she said. And I'm not always a sad person, some days I feel happy and then it works just the same; there's always something in it that fits exactly with my mood.

For me, that was like a real new start, and in other ways too it was as though I'd begun a whole new chapter in my life. This lady's daughter was around the same age as me and as well as having children she had a brother who was in prison. One day she asked me if I'd go with her when she visited with him. I'd told her I'd been incarcerated myself and she said she would understand if I wasn't inclined. It was kind of strange; I'd never thought I'd see the inside of a prison again and I'd never wanted to but on this occasion there was sort of something inside of me told me to go. So I did, and when we were sitting at the table with him her brother pointed out a prisoner there who he said had been inside a long time and no one came to see him, not ever. He called him over and introduced us: the man was Curtis and that's how I met him and I really took to him straight away. I could tell he was like me, a very shy sort of a person, and he talked very nicely and sincerely and in a nice straightforward way. I thought it would be really neat if he and I got along; so about a week after I'd met him I wrote him a letter saying would he like us to correspond. I've never in my whole life done anything like that before, I mean approached a man. I've always waited for them to make the first move. But I hadn't ever met a man who I liked immediately so much, so I guess that was what made me bold.

The correspondence between us went real well. Curtis said no one had written him in years and he'd forgotten how to write letters: he said he hoped I'd forgive him if he didn't express things well and made a load of mistakes. If he did I didn't notice it: he seemed able to put his thoughts down on paper better than I could, because he was always so direct and simple in the way he said things. That made it a whole lot easier for me to write to him and express my own thoughts too. We had a lot in common with each other: I don't mean about our prison experiences because we didn't write about them, but in how we looked at things, and of course most of all in our religion.

He read his Bible a lot because he was studying to be ordained. But I liked it too that he didn't have any crazy notions about that. He said he didn't know why he was doing it, except he was certain he knew he had to, it was God's will and the Lord would reveal to him in His own good time what His purpose was. He was always so enthusiastic about his studies: he told me and wrote me about them and it was like we were sharing a big experience together. It was clear to me Curtis was a good and sincere man. After not very long I thought of him as a true friend and someone I could really open my heart to.

I started to go regularly to see him on my own: and when I did I wasn't nowhere as shy with him as I'd thought I would be. He was shy but he was always so friendly and polite I never had the feeling from him I'd always had with other men, which was really all they wanted was the same thing. When I told him about Lionel he said one day he'd like to meet him if that was possible, so next time I took him along. It was a great success, they really liked each other. That night when we got home while I was tucking Lionel in bed he said to me "That was a nice man you took me to meet today Mom, is he my daddy?"

From what he'd said about his situation to me, it was clear Curtis thought he was going to stay in prison a very long time still. So it was a huge big surprise for both of us the day I went to visit with him and he told me he'd been given a date for his parole: I was so pleased, I did, I threw my arms around him and kissed him. We'd never done that before but it seemed like it was quite absolutely natural. When he asked me would I marry him when he was free I didn't have any hesitation, not even for one second: I said of course I would, and that's what we did, the very next day after he came out.

Gosh it's hot isn't it, should I make us some iced coffee or tea? Then we can go on and talk some more about things if you want.

That we've both been in prison for committing the same kind of crime, it's a help sometimes, yes and no. What I did and what Curtis

did, the result was a person finished up dead; but that's about the only
similarity there is between them. Mine was only a one-off kind of a
thing, it happened because of a series of domestic circumstances in my
life that I don't imagine would be repeated ever again. No one can be
certain about anything, but I'm as confident as anyone could be they
won't. Even if they ever were to somehow, I don't think I'd react to
them as I did, I mean not in that same way.

I think that's because a whole lot of things have made me stronger
in character: I've been through real deep troughs of sorrow and despair, but there's two things have helped me survive and come out of
them a better person. They've been one discovering the Bible, and two
meeting Curtis and being married with him. Living here next to our
church and working in the center have made a big difference too.
Straight away when we came Curtis was honest with everyone we met,
talking to them and saying where he'd been and what it was he'd done
time for. Everyone knew everything about him: his background when
he was a kid, what sort of a person he'd been, what happened with the
old lady and how he caused her to die. He said he wanted it like that:
and everyone in the church gave him immediate acceptance because of
his truthfulness about it and remorse.

I couldn't find the courage to do the same as he did though, not at
first. I was anxious about it, I didn't want everyone to know I'd been
incarcerated and why. I had to learn from him the strength not to hide
and to be completely open and honest with everyone. It took time; I
even said things to Curtis like I'd be happier if we went to live some
place else where everyone didn't want to know so much about us or
need to know so much about me. He was very gentle and patient and
understanding, and as time went by I found I was less afraid, and that
was only because of his love and support. It was because of the mem-
bers of our church too and the way they responded to me. When I
went to work at the center there was a lady there I was real scared of, I
didn't want her to find out what I'd done. Curtis said the best way to
handle it would be to find a time to be alone with her and then tell it
all to her at once, in every detail. When the opportunity came, I took

it. In spite of my apprehensions I confessed to her everything about myself: she listened to it all very calmly and when I'd finished she kissed me and thanked me for telling her and said it was very brave of me. She said she'd like me to know that as far as she was concerned, I was one of God's children just exactly the same as anyone else. Everyone in the church has been the same: now I'm not frightened of anyone finding out. Most everyone knows about me and they all treat me in that selfsame way.

There's just one thing I haven't worked through yet in myself: that's a feeling of bitterness I still have inside of me about my incarceration. This is the one big way Curtis and my feelings are different. He talks about prison being a time for him when his life turned around and he found a way to fulfillment and truth. He says it was God giving him an opportunity to redeem himself. I don't think anyone would argue with that, that's how it was for him; if anyone can be improved by the experience of long-term imprisonment, Curtis sure is an example of it. But I'm not; prison did me harm because it put so much that's bad and negative inside me.

My experiences with my father and with my husband Chuck and the other guy, they all made me very bitter towards men: and I don't mean only just those men but towards all mankind. They made me look on women as victims in a man's world. I remember at my trial how my anger used to rise when I heard them talk about Chuck as "the victim" of my attack, because I didn't see it that way at all. I said I hadn't worked through this and I haven't: there's part of me still sees it that way, that it was me who was the victim, not him. Losing my baby and being sent into prison added to that feeling as well. It seemed then and it still seems now to have been unfair in every way.

I don't know what they should have done with me instead; only I'd have thought I needed something else much more than punishment, and it was help. But my attorney was male, the district attorney who prosecuted me was male, and of course the judge was male too. I don't think it's possible ever for a man to appreciate how a woman sees things because their minds work in a different way, like in for instance if it's a case of infidelity: a lot of women will forgive a man that and they agree when they talk about it among themselves that that's the way men are. I've heard many of them in prison talking like that. But I don't know many men who'll forgive their wife infidelity, specially if they haven't first been unfaithful to her themselves.

There was a feeling everywhere among the women I was in prison with that in most instances it was men who'd put them there. Not just in the legal sense either, I mean a whole lot of them put the blame for them being there on men, as well as the men who mostly operate the legal mechanics of it. That was why it was a breeding ground for feminism and lesbianism. If you got entangled with another woman, you weren't going to let yourself in for the same amount of misery or the same sort of it if things started to go wrong as you would be if it was a man.

The Bible says you should forgive those who persecute you and despitefully use you, but I have to admit there are times when these feelings take over in me and I find it very hard to. I know it doesn't apply to all men—it's not true of Curtis, he's a fine and good man— but as soon as I say that I'm mentally adding on the thought in my mind that he's an exceptional man, very few men are like him.

That's one way which our experience of incarceration was different: neither of us have the same basic feeling about its value. Sometimes I get quite sharp about it too, especially when Curtis makes a comment about the benefit of it. If there are other people present it's hard for me not to say that isn't my own feeling about it.

That's what I mean when I say both us having undergone it isn't always a help to our understanding of each other and you could almost say it was a hindrance. He's understanding and sympathetic about the way I feel and I know it's a fault in me, but it sometimes leads me into very bad moods. He handles it well, because he can remember how it was for him when he was inside, he knows the sort of withdrawal from people you want. He went into the same sort of periods when no one from outside communicated with him and he thought he wasn't ever going to come out. Sometimes he talks about those. Then it's my turn to try and struggle to understand how it was for him because I never did: I was always full of anger and burning conviction I shouldn't be there.

I think where it's a help most is we both of us know what it's like to have people pass judgment on you for what you've done and can't undo. There's one other thing that binds us close too: we both know that kind of blanket feeling of loneliness that suddenly affects you and it seems to have no reason and to come from nowhere. When it happens with either of us we don't need to ask what's the matter: we know exactly what it is and the despondency in it, and how you can't do anything to make it go away, you just have to wait until it goes. It's a hard thing to live with in another person. It's natural to want to try and lift them out of it, you feel a failure if you can't, but we don't do that, we don't take it that way. It would be harder to handle it like that if you hadn't yourself been there.

But I know these are problems of adjustment to each other, as well as to the world around. I know God will help us with them like He's already done with other things. He brought us together and that was a sign He had a purpose for us. If He tests us I'm not afraid nor is Curtis. Already God's brought a new daddy into his life for Lionel; that's something very good, and I can't imagine there could be anything better for him than to have a home and a real family to grow up in. Maybe soon we'll have a brother or sister for him as well—that's something we both want and it'd make all our lives complete if we did.

Oh my, look what time it is! They'll be wondering at the center where I've got to, I guess I'd better go. The time's gone so fast hasn't it? I never knew I could talk that much. I hope it hasn't been a bore for you.

ECLECTIC, IF THAT'S THE RIGHT WORD

CARRIE HAMMICK

Gentle voiced and sturdy, with trimly bobbed blond hair and cornflower blue eyes she sat on a beach lounger by the window of her twelfth-floor apartment sipping from a soft-drink can and looking out relaxedly over the city on a cool summer's evening.

I'm thirty-eight: I did eighteen years in prison and came out a little over seven months ago. When I wake up in the mornings sometimes, I think I'm still there; for a minute I don't know where I am and that I've got to get out of bed and wash and dress of my own volition and go off to work. I listen out for the bell with my eyes closed, waiting for it to ring getting-up time.

I did murder and was sentenced to twenty years to life for it but I'm out on parole. When I was first released I thought Where have all the flowers gone? My youth, what happened to it, where's it been? But there was a kind of detachment about the question, more that than sorrow. I don't feel sorry for myself, I had one hell of a good time before, when I was a girl. I'll have one again too: things are shaping up good. I've a boyfriend, a job, I've still got looks, I'll make out. I should do, at my age. We all do, we're women of the world.

I was born a Catholic; whether I'm still one now I don't really know. My family were religious, my parents and both my sisters, we all went every Sunday to mass. I always felt different from them somehow though: what it was was I never had a strong sense of sin. I was a sinner as much as or more than most, but I never felt bad about it, somewhere along the line I missed out on guilt.

We were a close family and in lots of ways we still are, even if they live in Philadelphia and I live here. Until his retirement my father was a professor of English at a university, and my mother was an executive in a telephone company until she had to leave a few years back because of poor health. It added up to we had money and a good living standard: I come from a stable background, I'd not be an example of what happens to kids from a broken or deprived home. I had a good education too: I could have gone from high school on to college if I'd wanted. If I hadn't got into the drug habit early I might have.

I experimented with everything: marijuana, heroin, cocaine, you name it I tried it. I was eclectic, if that's the right word. Other people use alcohol or tobacco or whatever, and that's acceptable, but those who use drugs to get their kicks, they're considered way way down there. Addicts, junkies—they're called every sort of name, and suitable cases for treatment, everybody's trying to find out all the time why why why. Is it because they're weak, they had bad childhoods or something like that; what can we do to help them, to save them from themselves? Well that's crap: crap's all that is, crap that's all. Speaking personally as someone who used drugs regularly, it was because I liked them, that's why. I went on a prison program to get me off the habit and so okay I don't use them anymore, but that doesn't mean I have to say being on them did me harm. It didn't, no way. It'd be like me saying I'm not a Catholic because I've realized it's a harmful religion; I was only one because I couldn't see the error of my ways. If I've given it up it's because maybe I've grown out of it, I've found some other faith or no faith, I don't need the Catholic one anymore. Well it's the same with drugs: I've grown out of them and don't need them now, that's all. They should be decriminalized too: that would reduce crime since no one would be making money from dealing in them anymore.

I'd say I was hooked from twelve, or at the latest from thirteen. How I got onto them was through a relative, a good friend of the family, my uncle Rusty let's say he was called. He was one of my father's brothers: I was thirteen and he was twenty-three, and we smoked together and then went on further, on to other things. He often came to visit us weekends and times, he had a car and a good job and he wasn't married and he liked classical music and so did I. He was a nice guy: we used to go around together, he took me to concerts and theaters and movies and up to the mountains where he taught me how to ski. When anyone ribbed him about not having a girlfriend and being married, he always made a joke of it. He said he was waiting for me. In front of them with a laugh straight into my parents' faces, he told them he was waiting for me.

Well he wasn't: he wasn't waiting I mean. I wasn't, either: from when I was thirteen on, we had sex together, often, wherever and whenever we could. At my house when no one was there, at his apartment, when we went out in his car, just everywhere. And he may have been ten years older, but he didn't seduce me; if anything, to begin it was me seduced him. I didn't feel bad about it nor did he: it was fun, it was always what we most wanted to do. Like I said, I never had feelings that it was sin: how could it be when it was so good? For the both of us it was living life to the full. Then when drugs started to come into it, that gave it a lift even more. The guy was good for me and to me, and I was for him. Some people might say it was unusual and wrong because it was against the law, it was perverted, all that kind of thing. But I'd say no it wasn't, not for us, no way, not at all.

When I look back at it now twenty-five years afterwards, the only regret I might have is it didn't go on more. For a thirteen-year-old I don't think I was sexually precocious either, that's something else too with which I wouldn't agree. I was just like any other girl that age in my feelings: all I did was not rein them in. I wasn't a flirt and I wasn't promiscuous because he was the only one. And I wasn't so young I didn't have control of feelings and let him take advantage of me. I knew what I was doing, just exactly I did: I wasn't in love with him but I wanted sex and I enjoyed it, not with anyone but only with him.

So you have the picture, or I hope you have, right? A thirteen-year-old girl, not an oddity, bright at school and from a happy family home, having a love affair for want of a better term with an older man, and regularly using drugs. In a word, the all-American girl. Some would say no that's not possible, there's no way it could have been like that, her parents or someone would have known. Answer: They didn't; you can live your life in two parts or on two levels, both at the same time. So long as you're happy in yourself with it, those in one half needn't know anything about the other one.

"So long as you're happy" is the important part, though, and by the time when I was just fifteen, I wasn't happy with it anymore. I didn't want to hurt my parents. They'd been good to me, they'd never done anything wrong, they'd always given me a good home, but I was restless, I needed to break out from the domestic circle a while. The way I saw it there was only one thing I could do, and that was tell my parents how it was with me, and that meant they'd have to know about Rusty too. I worried about having to do it, but I think I knew whether they understood or not they wouldn't ever want a break with me. And that's just how it was though naturally they asked me had I worked out all the angles and implications that there were. I said yes, even if it wasn't strictly true: what I told them was only the half of it after all, because I didn't feel I could go all the way. I told them about me and Rusty of course, and because he'd always said that he was waiting for me it wasn't such a shock. The joke had become real but I think they'd half known for a while already that it was true.

What I didn't tell them was about the drugs. I couldn't. I thought being from a previous generation they'd find it too hard to take, and though it wasn't giving me any problems I knew it'd worry them. Rusty's job was with a farm insurance company and a transfer vacancy came up, so we went out west to Oakland, California. He'd been there once on vacation and liked it a lot, and when I got there I did too. The one thing we did level absolutely with my parents about though was we told them we were going to live together first and not get married yet, because of our age difference and we wanted to see how it worked out. Being the folk they were, they never lifted an eyebrow.

Our first home in Oakland was in a trailer park. For months we were happy and everything was fine. We never fought, we lived all the time for each other, and it was bliss. Rusty had the kind of job where he could take time off more or less when he wanted so long as he made it up. We did a lot of riding around, laid on the beach in the sun or swam in the bay. We'd have looked like any other happy young couple, and that's just how we were.

In the first year I got pregnant, and our baby daughter Tracey was born the day after my sixteenth birthday. There were no complications, neither for me nor for her. They try to scare you about drugs with telling you what you're doing to your child if you're on them while you're carrying it. I'm not saying none of it's true, but I wasn't ever a heavy user and nothing went wrong. People have this picture from TV and the movies that an addict's someone who never washes and has long straggly hair and can't manage her own life, never mind a child's. I wasn't that way; I was always clean and tidy and well fed and so was my little girl. If things hadn't happened that happened, everything would have gone along fine.

What it was was Rusty had an accident in his car: he crashed it trying to avoid an out-of-control truck on the freeway, and he was hospitalized. He had a broken arm and two cracked ribs and he needed an operation. I had to tell them for his safety's sake he was a drug user and after the surgery there were complications. He wanted to get out of the hospital and come home to me and Tracey, and he did it too soon: he was weak and ill and the treatment costs were enormous and used up all our insurance. His job was a two-thirds commission one so our income got low. Financially we were going down and down until we reached the point where we had no alternative but for me to find work and him stay home and look after Tracey.

I didn't have anything in the way of qualifications or experience selling and all I could get was a low-paid job in a video rental store. With all the bills we had and Rusty's small income, soon we were having a very hard time. There were long periods in the day when I was alone in charge of the store, so I started to take cash once in a while from the till. The owner's checking system didn't seem too smart and I thought it'd be easy to get around: I looked at it I was only taking a loan and would pay it back when I could.

It was three weeks at the most that's all before I was caught. The store owner wasn't as simple as I'd thought: he sent one of his buddies in to make a rental and I didn't record the payment, I kept the cash myself instead. He fired me the very next day. I offered to make restitution if he'd give me time though I didn't know how I was going to do it, and at first I thought he'd accept because he said he'd let me know. What he was doing was checking the accounts and totaling up; two weeks later he showed up at our home with a detailed sales check and said I owed him two thousand dollars or more. Rusty and I didn't have that kind of money or anything like it. The guy said well we could pay it off at a hundred a week, but if we didn't keep the payments up he'd prosecute.

I knew chances of getting some other job would be zilch and we couldn't see Rusty getting himself back to work in quite a while. So we talked it over and the way the situation was, there was only one alternative we could see: to deal in drugs till things got better. There was no other way we were going to pay off our debts, no way at all. And we decided it'd make more sense if I was the one that did it rather than Rusty. If he was busted for it, that would mean a prison sentence for sure and after that he'd never be able to get any kind of a job ever, not of a decent sort.

So I went into it on a small scale and it stayed that way for three years. I bought, and we disciplined ourselves to use that little bit less than we had been doing, and I sold the rest. This is another instance you won't get a full picture from the media of a drug dealer's world. They portray it always as sleazy and sneaky, they don't ever show you some other kind of side. The people I traded with, both buying and selling, were mostly people of our own sort: white and decent and middle class. A lot of them lived right there on the trailer parks; some of the others who didn't had real nice homes. They weren't crazed junkies who'd do anything for a fix: they were steady users, reliable, with good living standards, not harming anyone, just following their own way of life.

It took three years for me to clear our debts but I did, I paid off every one: the guy I'd stolen from at the video store, our insurance bills, everything. I didn't get involved with drug rings and big-time operators either, just went steadily along. Then I became pregnant again: I had a second daughter who was named Noreen and it meant once more we started having a hard time. The main reason was Rusty's health. The medical bills kept on coming and just when we'd thought we were on the up, once more we started going down. The only way out was I had to get further into the scene. I didn't want that because of some of the characters you get involved with, but I had no choice. I had to do it and that's how I ended up part of a big-time ring.

I don't know how much you're familiar with drug dealing, maybe not a lot I'd guess. Tuesday I was telling you about how I got into it deeper than I ever wanted, right? I'll go on from there; if there's anything you're not clear about it, ask me and I'll stop and explain. I was saying I wasn't my own boss anymore, I wasn't in control of my life, I was putting myself at risk. The more people you're involved with and know about you, the more chance someone'll be an informer among them or someone'll blackmail you and all that sort of thing. So I didn't like it and I didn't want to be part of it but I had to be.

The big risk was the one I hadn't taken into account enough. When it came at first I thought I could handle it, but I was wrong, because from then on my life took a real bad turn. I had a man I loved very much, who was Rusty, I had two lovely kids, Tracey and Noreen who we both adored, and as well as getting out of debt we saved enough money to put down the deposit on a ground-floor apartment near the beach. The earnings potential was greater when you are in an organization and not just operating on your own, but money's not everything, and other things were totally spoiled.

There was a guy who was in the consortium with me, and one way and another we were thrown together quite a few times. Now and again you have to travel quite some distance to get new supplies, or make a delivery to someone, and a time or two it involved being away a night. We'd stay at a hotel and make like we were a businessman and his secretary, and at first it was all regular and above board and we each had a separate room. He was a good-looking guy and I liked him, and I know now I should have been careful. One way to do that would have been to tell Rusty exactly how the situation was from the start. Only I didn't. If I had to be away a night I didn't tell him any detail about who I was going with; I said "we" were going somewhere, like four or five people were involved. I guess it was because I had the feeling if he knew it was only me and one other guy he'd start thinking things. Maybe I was thinking those things myself too, that they might happen, and I wasn't telling Rusty because I half hoped they would. That's what a psychologist would say.

Well, inevitably they did. About the third or fourth time we were away he came to my room and we spent the night together. I've not pretended: sex was something I enjoyed. I was twenty, I'd been with Rusty seven years, and maybe doing it once in a while with this one other guy gave it a little extra spice. Illicit too, I enjoyed that. Like I said, I've always been short on a sense of sin. Guys anyway do it don't they, all the time? Away from their wives in a hotel for a night with their secretaries: what they're thinking of is going to bed with them. When a woman does it she's a whore they say, but when it's a man it's harmless and just fun.

I thought I was in control of it and it didn't alter my feeling for Rusty and the kids. I didn't want a breakup or to be permanently with the other guy, I was just happy to go with it once in a while. But he wasn't: he got more and more fixed on me. He had a wife and he started giving me all the stuff about how unhappy he was with her and he wanted to spend the rest of his life with me. And his physical demands were increasing all the time: afternoons after we'd done some deal or other instead of taking me home he'd drive with me out to the country and we'd go in the woods and he wouldn't take me back again until we'd made love. But don't get the idea he was pressuring me every time because he wasn't. I liked it that he felt that way about it sometimes, other times I didn't mind. But sometimes I definitely did, and the more insistent he was about me leaving Rusty, the more I wanted to hold him off and the harder it became.

Then one day he told me I had to choose: either I had to break from Rusty, or he'd tell him what'd been going on. Rusty was sick and he had a weak heart; I was scared what that would do to him and what would become of the kids, and anyhow I didn't want to leave Rusty. When you've been together as long as we had, that would almost be like having a divorce. I told the guy I needed a couple of days to think it over and arrange things. I thought that'd keep him quiet a while and give me time to work out what I was going to do.

From Monday to Friday he left me alone, and we'd agreed to meet that day at four in the afternoon. We had a drink in a bar at the beach and I said everything was fixed, I'd told Rusty and I was leaving him the next day. I suggested we celebrate by driving up into the hills overlooking the bay where there were trees and a stream: we'd been there before and it was an ideal place where we could be on our own. He fell for it—an hour later we were there. It was an isolated place on a ledge like a high-up shelf of grass on the edge of a ravine. We made love, then I took out my .25 from my purse and I shot him six times. I pushed his body over the cliff and it fell down out of sight something like two hundred feet below. I was sure no one would ever find him. I drove his car back down to the beach and after I'd wiped it down to remove any fingerprints I left it on a parking lot along with a few hundred other vehicles so before anyone noticed it it'd be several days. Then I took a cab to another part of the beach, then another one to someplace else, and last a third cab back home.

I gave the kids something to eat and put them to bed: Rusty and I watched TV for a while, and then we went to bed too. To me that was it, it was done, it was over; I didn't feel bad about it at all. If the guy hadn't been so pushy and tried to make me do what he wanted, if he'd just backed off, he'd have still been alive today. I did what I had to do and if I hadn't been very unlucky people wouldn't ever have known. His body deep down in a ravine, his car where it wouldn't attract attention—it should all have turned out okay: people disappear every day without saying to anyone where they're going. He'd have been notified as missing to the police but that'd have been it: life could have gone on for Rusty and the kids and me again just the same way as before.

But what I had was a real bad stroke of luck; you couldn't call it anything else, no way. The very next day two kids came from nowhere with their parents to have a picnic on the other side of the ravine: they climbed all the way down to the bottom of it and found the body. Then all hell broke loose, it really did, all over the local radio and TV. The police knew the guy was in a drug ring. They didn't know I was, but they started to put the heat on some of the others and I knew in the end it'd lead them to me. One thing I never had to doubt about Rusty was whatever I did, he'd always look after me, so I didn't hesitate and told him what I'd done. The only thing I didn't tell him was how far I'd gone with the guy. I just said he'd driven me out to the place and tried to force me to have sex with him and I'd panicked and killed him in self-defense.

Like I knew he would be, Rusty was right on my side: he said the best thing we could do was disappear and go as far away as we could. So far as I knew no one knew my real name. I always made out we were married and Rusty's name was mine. I told a neighbor we were going away a while, and I thought I was safe and it'd all blow over in time.

So we packed up the car and the kids, and next morning we took off in the early hours. We'd decided to go to my parents, and we stopped off in the middle of the morning to call them. I said we were having a vacation and were bringing the kids to see them, and we'd be arriving in a couple of days. When we got there the police were ahead of us: there was a reception committee of them waiting for us at my parents' home. I don't remember doing it, but I must have sometime told the neighbor I was from Philadelphia, that's the only way we could have been traced and found so soon.

I talked and I talked and I talked; I told them I'd killed the guy, and there was no way out for me, I knew. They said they were going to charge Rusty with being an accessory, which in a way he was, but after the act. He'd had nothing to do with the killing, which finally they agreed. He got three years, I drew twenty to life. My parents took over our kids and the way I saw it then, my life was at an end. It was too, for all that part.

It had all been based on one thing: drugs. In prison I went on a rehab program, which was long and hard. Everyone knows you can get them in there if you want them, and I did for a year, but then I decided I'd make a fresh start. What brought me to decide it was that a year into his sentence, Rusty died. And that wasn't the finish of a chapter, it was the ending of a book or like a door being closed. They helped me a lot in prison with it, his death I mean. I had counseling and psychotherapy and if I thought life wasn't worth living for myself, after a while I felt for my daughters' sake I must go on. I asked my parents to keep them in touch with me and they did: they brought them to see me once every three months without fail. That made a difference: it helped me through, watching them grow up into fine healthy girls. Tracey's twenty-two now and married to an advertising agency man in New York; Noreen's eighteen and at college, studying to be a social anthropologist. When I'm more sure of myself I'll move east to be nearer them, but my plan is to take a year to rehabilitate myself outside first.

I can't say much about prison. I don't like to talk about it, it's too close still. But while I was there I learned two things. One was the law because I studied for a degree: I haven't got it yet but I will next year. The other was some humility and tolerance, how not to put what I want first all the time. Prison's a leveler: I'm not recommending it as an experience everyone'd be better for, but it has brought someone like me in contact with people who're the sort I wouldn't meet outside and probably wouldn't have known about or cared. Blacks and Hispanics particularly, they're overrepresented in prison in our great multiracial society we're so proud of, the U.S. of A. I never knew any before, not on a day-to-day level of living among them. In a way it was that that led me to first take up an interest in law. So many people from minority groups knew nothing about the legal system or what their rights were. I thought a way of helping was not just to feel sorry for them but to learn something practical, so I started to read all I could find. And after that I enrolled for the degree course I'm on.

Meanwhile now through people I wrote to I've a job as a paralegal with a firm of criminal lawyers in the city here, where it's just as I thought: where we are, most of the people who come into our office are black and are having a run-in with the law. The system's tilted against them and they don't know how to defend themselves. And I enjoy it, it's good to feel I'm doing something for other people for a change.

I'D LIKE A NICE
WHITE OLDER MAN

MIZ GREEN

*Plump and laughing, dark skinned and with mischievously twin-
kling big brown eyes, she sat in a typing chair in the parole
officer's room with her legs stretched out in front of her. She
wore knee-length boots, a short tight black skirt, and a multicolored
sweater patterned with circles of blue and red and green on a white
background. A wisp of frilly white lace tied back her hair. Her voice was
deep and slow: she drew on a cigarette, tilting back her head and blowing
the smoke out languorously into the air.*

Wow, that's sure a difficult thing to do to describe yourself—you
mean who I am, how I look, or what? Everything, anything? Wow!
Well okay then here goes, I'll try. My name is Miz Green: usually I like
to keep it that way, you know, formal, but for you I'll make an exception, you can call me Anthea okay? I'm a young black woman twenty-
nine years of age, I'm five eleven in height, I weigh one hundred eighty
pounds, but I'm a big girl and it's all nicely spread around. My mea-
surements are thirty-nine to forty, thirty-three waist and hips forty-
two. Someone once told me I had a figure like a painting by a guy
called Reuben but I've never seen one of his so I wouldn't know. Let's
see . . . what else? Well, we're sitting in Mr. Samprella's office because he's out of town; we're here because he's my parole officer and
I'm on parole. I was sentenced to ten years to life, and I was a good
girl during my incarceration so they released me when I'd done ten,
which was one year ago. I live on my own except for my mynah bird,

who's called Dominique, in a one-room apartment in that block which you can see over the road from that window there. That was found for me by Mr. Samprella and I have to obey his instruction to live where he says; my home's really the north of the city but he doesn't want to go back there yet a while. I do go there sometimes to see my ma, but I have to be back in my apartment here every night no later than nine. I think that's mighty hard on me because I was born and brought up in that neighborhood and that's the place all my friends and family are. Only he don't trust me.

My childhood would you like to know about, yeah? Okay, my background is I'm the youngest one out of six children, four girls and two boys. My pa was a factory worker. He left my ma a little after I was born so I've no recollection of him and where he is now nobody knows. My ma is a hardworking woman and always has been: she's educated and has certificates and stuff like that, and right now she works in the offices of the Transportation Department at City Hall. Me and her are pretty close and always have been, even after my crime. She came to see me whenever she could, but being so far for her to travel, that was just once or maybe twice a year. None of my other sisters and brothers has ever been in trouble, not one: you could say I'm the black sheep of the family cept there's not so much of the sheep. I'm not one for the flock; I value my independence, I go my own way.

From when I was a kid, I hung out with the boys. I didn't go for any of that skipping rope dancing and playing with dolls: I'd always sooner I was running around and climbing walls and generally making a nuisance of myself, from when I was very very young. I remember once I'd gotten into some kind of trouble and my ma said to me "Anthea" she said, "why don't you try behaving like a young lady for a change?" A young lady's sure something I've never wanted to be, not ever in my life. And behaving's never appealed to me either, it don't seem like living if you can't have no fun.

I wasn't no tomboy though, don't get me wrong: I liked being a girl, specially with boys. From early on I didn't go much on school, because my ma was working and my older sister was left in charge; only she had boyfriends and cars, so she didn't spend much time home. So what you've got to do if you want your own life is you've got to make your own life, if you know what I mean. I'm talking independence here: and independence well the first thing that that means is financial independence, right? So how does a girl get financial independence when she's fourteen? Well there's only one way. She has to get someone to look after her, right? So that's just what I did.

His name was Oliver and he was forty-four years of age: that's thirty years older than me which is a lot, a lot of people would say. Only if you like somebody, age don't matter at all, not one little bit. Besides I was a big strong girl and men like that, don't they? In a dark room I could have passed for twenty-one. And Oliver, he was the opposite, he looked very young for his age: he had all his own teeth and all his own hair, and in a dark room he could have passed for thirty-three. Besides, him and me we were made for each other, you know what I mean? Boys of my age were all silly and stupid, but Oliver was a man. In prison they give you all this psychological stuff, there was a woman there who was what's called a counselor and you know what she told me? She told me one day Oliver represented my missing father for me who I was looking for all the time. Well if you'll pardon the expression that's bullshit. Oliver wasn't like no father to me, he was my lover and that was what I wanted, not sitting on his knee while he read me fairy stories out of a book, you know what I mean? It was very sad what happened with Oliver and me eventually, but it didn't have nothing to do with wanting a father, no no no no.

He was very good-looking, he had a car and an apartment in a good neighborhood which is where I went to live. I told my ma I'd got a job working for a couple who wanted a nursemaid for their kids, and that was nearly true in a way, cept Oliver didn't have a wife and family, he lived on his own. But I did work at looking after him, I cooked for him and kept the apartment nice and everything. What he was was a drug dealer, but in a good class: some of the people he supplied, they were very well known. And this has to be said, he never took drugs himself, and he never gave them to me. He said I was a nice girl and a good girl, and he wanted me to stay that way; I respected him for that because he respected me.

He always treated me nice, very nice indeed: he brought me nice clothes and we lived in his apartment together almost a year. Then one night something terrible happened and he nearly got caught. I don't know the details of it except it was due to a snitch. Oliver got very angry about it and swore he'd kill the guy who had been responsible, but I don't think he did. I was glad of that because it would only have meant more trouble that's all. The guy did disappear though, and when the case came for trial after a long delay while the law tried to find him, it finally got thrown out because there wasn't sufficient evidence so Oliver stayed free.

But things got difficult for him then, I mean naturally, you know what I mean? He couldn't go back to selling drugs again because they were waiting to find a way of prosecuting him and he was under close surveillance all the time: so it looked like our standard of living would have to go down, but I didn't want that and neither did he. So we had to think of something else to make a living instead, which we did.

There's lots of reasons people go on drugs, and if you've got the habit, naturally you have to have money for it, that's obvious, right? And one of the things females will do to get easy money is what's called prostitution. If you know the right places to go find females that's on drugs, and you talk to them the right way, pretty soon you can build yourself a nice little business by the laws of supply and demand. Okay so that's what Oliver and me were able to do: we'd find a girl who had to have drugs and we'd promise to supply her regular so long as she supplied us regular with cash. That way everybody was satisfied. Oliver always took me along with him so the girl could see everything was regular and above board: often I could say things to a girl that he couldn't that'd keep her calm and reassured. There was lots I could tell her like where to go and how to behave, how to talk a john up and what sort to avoid. It was all strictly legitimate, and I was kind of their contact with Oliver and his courier and help all the time.

You're sure it doesn't bother you me keeping on smoking cigarettes? I should have asked you first. Pardon me for not; one thing you
forget when you're incarcerated is good manners you know? But if
you'd not like me to go on then say to me "Anthea please stop smoking those cigarettes Anthea will you please?" and I will, I'll stop
right away.

Okay where was I, about me being like Oliver's manager for him
out in the field. How I knew all the stuff that I was able to tell the girls,
well that was by my own experience of course. I'd done a little prostituting myself from when I was twelve. I mean nothing serious, but I
knew what I was talking of if a girl hadn't done it before. It's a good
way of earning money I think—in fact I'd say one of the best ways
there is if you're sensible about it, you know how I mean? You get so
you can sum up a john by looking at him and know if he's trouble and
just say politely no thank you, you're not that sort of a girl. I know
there's men who don't want anything rough either; if a man does then
he should go find someone else, that's how it's always seemed to me.

I don't know there's much else to say about that part of my life.
It's been interesting for me visiting with you. Like Mr. Samprella said
Tuesday's always a good day. We can use his office because he goes out
seeing clients so he's not here. Tuesday's a good day for me too: I go to
my aerobics class at the hall over the street, so if you want we can talk
some more next Tuesday. Shall I come at the same time, will that
be okay?

Well what I'd like for us to talk about this time is how I came to
commit my crime.

It's very sad for me to think about it: it caused me to lose the best
man in my life, which was Oliver and it was all down to what I did. I
mean I know it was very bad and while I was in prison serving my
sentence I was hoping all the time I'd have a letter saying he'd forgiven
me, or he'd come and see me and we could talk and then I'd ask him
could we try again. But it didn't happen. Now he's married and lives
somewhere in Florida I think; I don't suppose I'll ever see him again
and that hurts it really does, it really makes me sad.

We had a good time together always, him and me. One of the
things we liked best was going to a disco club which was called the
Black Tulip which was named after a famous film. We used to go there
every week on a Saturday. It had a nice atmosphere and you'd always
have a good class of person there because all the drinks and the food
and everything, they were all high priced and you had to be a member
to get in. We'd dance and we'd have maybe a salad with tunafish and
one or two drinks and then we'd go home.

One night there was a man there and his name I don't know.
Oliver knew him from somewhere and he invited him to have some
food with us, and we all had a good time. Then this guy said he had a
business proposition he wanted to put to Oliver, but he said it was
private and he'd like it if they could go to a room some place upstairs
in the club and have their talk there. I was sore at Oliver that he agreed
to that, taking me for a night out dancing and then leaving me sitting
all on my own. The guy'd promised what he had to talk to Oliver
about would take ten minutes, but they were gone for more like an
hour. If a girl's sitting by herself in a place of that sort, naturally
there's some men will stop by and ask her can they buy her a drink or
something. And when you've refused offers six or seven times and
you're getting angry like I was, there comes a time you agree. That's
just what eventually happened with a guy: he'd had too many drinks
himself, and before long he was sitting close to me and putting his
hand on my thigh. I told him I didn't like that and I was there with a
friend who'd gone to the toilet and he'd be coming back soon. I don't
know how long it was Oliver wasn't there, but of course what happened was when he did come back it was just at the moment when
this guy was touching my leg again and Oliver saw it going on. He was
all for having a fight with this guy whose name was Alfredo by the
way. I didn't think this was a good idea because Alfredo was bigger
than he was and I think he could have caused him harm. Besides, it
wasn't that sort of a club where people had brawls: the atmosphere
was nice and peaceful, it wasn't no rough-and-tumble place at all.

So what happened then was Oliver said we were leaving and we
were going home. I didn't want to, I wanted us to all have another

drink and make up and be friends, only Oliver was in a real bad temper about it and said we must leave. When we got back to our apartment we had our first quarrel ever, because Oliver kept on and on calling me names, and me him I suppose. I hated that, I'm not a quarrelsome sort of a person, I just like things to be easy and slow. And because I was trying to calm him about Alfredo I said things the wrong way, so Oliver then started accusing me that I liked Alfredo more than him and things of that sort. My, it was awful, it really was, and it ended with Oliver telling me I should pack all my things up and go. He was still the same way next morning as well—I thought he might have calmed down only he just seemed worse that's all. I said I didn't have no money and no place to go, so he took his wallet out and threw the money that was in it onto the floor and said I should take it and never come back no more. He said he was going for a walk: he'd be away for one hour he said, and when he returned he didn't want to find me there.

That was a very cruel thing to do to someone, you know, I was really upset he should treat me that way as though I was dirt. But I thought maybe if I did go he'd miss me and after a couple of days if I called him he'd say for me to come back to him again, which I would have if things had worked out that way. Anyway I packed up my bag and I did what Oliver'd said, I took the money and I left and was gone before he was back. I walked around a while to try and think what to do: it was June and summer and the weather was sunny, so I spent most of the day in the park. In the evening I went to a restaurant and had myself something to eat, and then I booked in for the night at a small hotel. I didn't go out of my room, I watched the movie on TV a while, then before I went to bed I called up the apartment because I was lonely and I wanted to talk to Oliver real bad but no one answered the phone. I thought maybe he'd gone to the disco club, so I called there too; they said he hadn't been in, and I said if he did come would they please ask him to call me and I gave them the hotel number where I was and then I went to bed. I couldn't sleep because I was so upset, and when the telephone rang at two in the morning, my heart gave a leap because I thought it was Oliver and it meant things might work out okay after all.

Only it wasn't Oliver, it was Alfredo. He was asking me what happened and where was I, he was worried what might have happened to me after the night before. Least that's what he said. But I didn't believe him, he was the one that'd caused all the trouble in the first place and which was why Oliver and me had quarreled, because Alfredo didn't behave. I told him this, but I didn't tell him where I was cept I was in a hotel and I was leaving first thing next morning to find some place to live on my own.

Alfredo, you know, he was persistent that guy, he really was. The next morning when I was eating my breakfast in the diner just by the hotel, there he was all of a sudden standing there right in front of me. What he'd done was an hour earlier he'd called the number and when they said there was no reply from my room, he'd asked the switchboard operator the name of the hotel and come on right over to find me. I didn't like Alfredo that much and I should have told him right there and then to leave me alone and go away: but all I can say was I was still emotionally upset about Oliver, and you don't think straight when you're like that, you know what I mean?

So I didn't do what I should have, I did what I shouldn't have instead. Alfredo offered me a place to stay a while while I sorted out things and that's what I did. You know how it is when you're all mixed up and then along comes somebody who's nice to you and you're sad and lonely and on your own? And you have a few drinks together and you tell each other things and one thing kind of leads to another and before long you're in bed? Well, that's how it was: I didn't like him very much, but I felt I owed him, you know what I mean? I didn't look for some place else to go, he said there was no need. I was worried Oliver might hear, but you know also in a way I hoped that he did, and it'd make him jealous and he'd come round to Alfredo's place and drag me away.

Well that didn't happen, and that made me sad, and something else happened the next week, and that made me sadder still. A girl came round to the apartment one day asking for Alfredo when he was not there, and when I told her she looked me in the face and she said "Are you one of his girls?" That was such a shock to me I cannot describe: I got angry about it with her and I said "No I am not!" She said to me "Okay okay calm down. I am, I thought you must be too." So when he came back I had a big quarrel this time with Alfredo. He tried to soothe me, saying well I must know I was special to him, I was the one he lived with. But that didn't make me feel no better, it just made me despair. It was no use either, because then things got worse. He told me his plan; he told me I couldn't stay with him unless I went out to work.

Like I told you, I think a little prostituting is okay now and then, say if you need money for your drug habit or something like that. But to do it for a guy and he's going to live on it while he has a good time himself, to me that is not okay. If he's the one who wants the money, he's the one should lie on his back. So I said no I wasn't going to do that: and like I've told you as well, I didn't like the guy. It might have been different if I had, you know what I mean?

Well Alfredo he kept going on about it and going on about it, he just never stopped. And I'll tell you I was frightened of him, he scared me a lot. He wasn't no alcoholic, I'm not saying that, but he did drink more than he should and when he was like that it would make him violent in his talk and with his hands and he started slapping me about. He had a gun which he always carried too, and a knife as well. This was a very unhappy situation for me, to be living with a man I was so frightened of. It stayed that way two nights I think or maybe it was three; each time the quarrels and arguments we had took ugly turns, with him threatening me that if I didn't go out and earn money he'd throw me out on the street. And he wasn't like Oliver either—he wasn't the sort of guy to throw the cash in his wallet at me when he told me to go.

The last night was the night of the crime. What happened was he came back to the apartment and there was trouble like before. Only this time it was worse; he had a lot of drink inside of him and I could tell from the way he looked at me when he was telling me this was my last chance that he meant it, it was, he really did. I knew he meant it about my safety; he was ready to be going to do something to me that was really bad for me, I could tell. Then suddenly it was like he switched off, it was kind of strange and eerie like, you know? He stopped yelling at me and went very quiet, and he sat on the sofa and switched on the TV. He kept putting his face in his hands and screwing his eyes up like he couldn't properly see. He told me to make him something to eat and you know, I found that scary too: it was like he'd formed a plan in his mind, like a schedule of things in order he was going to do.

I went in the kitchen and rattled a few plates and stuff to sound like I was preparing a meal. I was thinking and thinking how to find a way to go out, you know without him come running after me and catching me and dragging me back. There was an old chair that was broken lying there by the kitchen wall in a corner: one of its legs was off and he was keeping it for repair. I thought well if I could just incapacitate him long enough to give me time to run out, then I'd be okay. So I took the chair leg and I held it behind my back like here and I came up behind him where he was sitting. My idea was I'd hit him over the head with it just the once to lay him unconscious, you know what I mean? With the TV on and everything he didn't hear me coming and he didn't turn round, so I could do it as I intended: I hit him over the head. Only then things went wrong and he just sort of fell forward off the couch onto the floor on his hands and knees. I hadn't hit him hard enough I guess; he just stayed there doing this, like a dog shaking its head. Then he kind of half turned around and looked at me, and he started trying to get up. I was scared what he'd do, so I went around where he was and I hit him again. Really he must, he must have had a really thick skull: I mean I'm built well and I'm strong, but however hard I hit him he just wouldn't stay down. I'd damaged him some way because there was blood coming out of his mouth, but I had to hit him six times I guess before he finally stayed still and fell on his back.

I hadn't meant to hit him so much; I'd thought it would be simple to lay someone unconscious, you know? And all that time he was laying there his eyes were still open; I didn't know if he was dead or conscious still, or what. And it flashed through my mind something I have read: that if a dead person has their eyes open, if you look into them it shows the reflection of the person who killed them there. I can't tell you, I was so afraid; I mean only just talking about it now so long after, I'm afraid to think about it, my hands start trembling—I mean look.

The thought he might come to life again and tell people who it was had done it to him, that was terrible. In the room there was a fold-down bed: you know the sort you pull down from the wall? I'd seen it a time or two and I knew it had a foam mattress on. So I let it down and took the mattress off it and put it on top of him to cover his face and tore it open and threw the filling of it everywhere around. There was a kerosene can in the kitchen which was used for the heater so I poured that on it and started a fire. I guess I must have been out of my head.

Then I ran out in the street and I took a cab. The only place I could think of to run to was my ma's. But that was a long journey over the north side of the city, so on the way I got calmer and started to think about things and I knew I couldn't go there. I told the taxi driver to forget it and take me to the nearest police station and I went in there and told them what I'd done. It was all very sad.

I was six months in custody awaiting my trial. At first they told me there'd be two counts on the indictment, homicide and attempted arson, only in return for me pleading guilty to the first one they agreed to drop the second one instead. I drew ten years to life, and I was nineteen years of age.

Only let me tell you you know what? Life in the correctional training facility for women, which is another name for prison, well it wasn't too bad. If you're a friendly person like me and you're not picky and quarrelsome all of the time, you can get along with the other girls there and you often have fun. In our dormitory where I was, there were six of us girls and we all got along fine: I was the organizer for the block and we had dances and discos and all kinds of things. You know you meet some real nice people in prison too, you really do. Like clever people who are studying for examinations and read books and can teach you things. I'm not clever enough myself to do that but while I was there I did, I made some really good friends. People think everyone who's incarcerated must be bad, but they're not: some of them are good, they've just been unlucky that's all. I wouldn't put myself in that category because what I did was bad, it was very bad it was. But some of those women and girls in there, they'd had such sad lives you wouldn't believe.

And you know when it came time for me to come out, I was really scared? You hear about these terrible muggings and rapes all the time that there are in the news, all the shootings and so on, you think the world isn't going to be a good place you know for a woman on her own. I mean there was that man killed all those prostitutes, did you read about him? I think that's terrible. Not all prostitutes are bad people, you can't see why he should kill them all like that.

What I do now for my living, well I'll tell you, right now times are hard. Mr. Samprella, I mean he's trying to get a job for me but not too many people are keen on employing someone like me, so I have to find ways of getting by. I don't see my family because like I told you he doesn't want me to go to that part of the city yet, but I have a feeling he will, he'll say it's okay for me before long. He says why don't I find a nice guy and marry him but I like to pick and choose and keep my freedom, you know? If I met Oliver again it would be different, but I don't think I ever will. He wrote me before my trial and said he never wanted to see me no more. I might meet someone else one day I suppose. I don't like men my own age. The sort I'd most like would be an Italian or a Frenchman or even an Englishman, someone white because I've had enough of black men for a while. I'd like a nice white older man, you know, someone who'd look after me and take care of me and would like a bit of romance themselves with a big strong black girl. If you meet someone like that tell him about me and give him my name.

III

HOPING SOME, AND THEN SOME MORE

THREE IMPRISONED
MEN

PRACTICING FOR THE PRIESTHOOD

DONALD MORRISON

*I*n the clatter and clamor of the prison dining hall he sat alone, as
far away from others as he could get, against the wall at the end of
the last of the long tables. Before beginning to eat he closed his
eyes, clasped his hands, and bowed his head over his paper plate, crossing
himself repeatedly while he whispered a litany of prayers. He ate the slab
of luncheon meat and the boiled carrots and potatoes mechanically,
chewing with a distant look in his eyes and a preoccupied frown. A short
slightly built man of nearly forty with a pale face and thinning hair, he
wore shabby dungarees and a blue-striped flannel collarless shirt.

Afterward in the sunshine in the compound outside he walked on his
own slowly round the inside of the razor-wire perimeter fence. When he
came to the steps at the entrance to the cell block he suddenly stopped
and turned.

Excuse me, will you be here tomorrow again as well? Would you
have any free time around noon? Could I come then and talk with you
a while, would that be okay?

No I don't know why, I don't think there was any special reason,
just a kind of a spur-of-the-moment kind of thing. I was a little
surprised at myself, it's not a thing I usually do, approach strangers I
mean. I hope you don't mind?

Who I am is Donald Morrison, and who he is, well he's a high
school graduate from the state of Arkansas and a former navy man.

He spent several years in the navy and then committed a murder for which he received a sentence of natural life imprisonment, which in our judiciary's terms means imprisonment for the rest of your natural life which ergo means forever. Does he expect to serve it? Yes. What else to tell you about him I don't really know. Let me think about it for a moment. He comes from what you could call a middle-class background, his father being a water engineer and he has a younger brother who is in business, in property or real estate as it's called. I would say that his early years were quite happy and normal and not in any way eventful: he was an average student, his grades were average to good as a rule, he didn't excel at anything but he was by no means at the bottom of the pile. From a very young age he always wanted to travel and see other countries in the world. He grew up during the Vietnam War but I don't know whether that's particularly significant or not. I would say at the time it didn't impinge: it was something happening in another country which was far away. You read about it, and you read about protests about it, but it didn't seem to have very much to do with you and you didn't have any strong feelings about whether it was right or wrong.

That's all I can say about him I think from an objective point of view. Perhaps I ought to mention that he was a lonely boy and didn't seem to be able to make many friends apart from one. This was his only real friend and his name was Ringle. He was in fact a dog, a mongrel dog, and he seemed to know exactly what my moods were without ever needing to be told. He would always fall in with whatever I wanted to do. If I wanted to sit by a stream and look in the water, Ringle would be happy sitting and just looking in the water too. If I wanted to run to the top of a hill Ringle would run very fast a yard or so ahead and somehow he knew where we were aiming to get was the top of the hill. He never made demands like wanting a stick to be thrown for him, but if a stick was thrown for him, he would dash off and bring it straight back.

I don't remember what became of him; in fact when I come to think about it now I'm not sure even if he was my dog. My memories aren't of him in the house ever, but rather of going out the back and whistling and Ringle would appear and the two of us would go off together everywhere. That's as objective as I can be about myself I think, in reference to when I was a young person. I was an ordinary boy with a dog, that's all.

I didn't leave school until I was eighteen and then I went straight into the navy where I was trained as a torpedo engineer. The torpedoes had nuclear warheads and I've since come to think that nuclear weapons are wrong and that warfare of all kinds is wrong, whatever the reasons or excuses given for it are. I'm now what would be called a convinced Catholic pacifist with firm convictions, but of course when I was in the navy I wasn't a Catholic or a pacifist. It's now a matter of great regret to me that I had anything to do with nuclear warheads or even the navy itself; I now consider that part of my life to have been very very wrong.

What I had joined the navy for didn't happen either: my ideas never came to fruition of traveling and seeing the world. After I was fully trained as a torpedo engineer I was moved on to one base camp where I trained young recruits, then to another one, then to another one after that and so on, and I never ever went to sea at all. I was mostly in camps on the western seaboard and during the whole of my service I never left the U.S.A.

I was what is called a sergeant instructor, and because of that I didn't mix with men of lower rank, nor was I accepted into the higher-up echelons of the officer rank either, so I spent most of my time on my own. I am a naturally quiet and shy person so I made no effort to look for friends. In my spare time I went to the movies a lot, and sometimes I would go out of camp to the nearest town and find a bar. I particularly liked what were called topless bars, where you sat at a table on your own and a waitress would come to serve you, and she would have no clothes on down to her waist and her breasts would be completely bare. I liked looking at half-naked women and some of the topless waitresses were very pretty girls. I was too shy ever to speak to any of them, I just looked at them, and if I could I found a table to sit at in a dark corner where I could have a drink and smoke a little pot. I never had more than two drinks in any one evening and I was not addicted to marijuana or pot as it's commonly called. That would be my description of a night out and I always found it pleasant and enjoyable.

I had never had a love affair or made love with a woman in any way until I was twenty-two, when I had my first and one and only love affair with a woman who was my senior in age by eight years. I met her in a coffee shop one morning in a small town when I was at the base there. I was reading the newspaper and eating a doughnut when she came and sat at my table and asked me did I have a cigarette to spare. I thought this was a strong thing for a well-dressed woman to ask from a man she didn't know and there was a vending machine in the smoking area she could have used, but she was obviously in a state of some distress and had asked because she had wanted to talk to someone and could see I was sitting by myself.

She was a very attractive woman who was well spoken and had thick red hair down to her shoulders and deep green eyes. I've never been to Ireland but she was in many ways my idea of what a beautiful Irish woman would look like. But her name was Barbara, and I understand that has no Irish connections at all, though I believe St. Barbara is supposed to be the patron saint of engineers. She was obviously very distressed about something, and before long she began telling me she was from Utah and had only recently come to live in Oregon, where she had no relatives or friends and knew no one at all. She had come with her husband to whom she'd been married for seven years, and he had recently taken up with another woman and started as a result being very cruel to her, hitting her and so on, and she showed me a number of bruises on her arm. I felt very sorry for her, and when she asked me if I would go back to her home with her I agreed. The reason she gave was that if her husband was there she'd be frightened to go in the house on her own so she'd drive away again and I wouldn't in any way be involved. I left my car in the parking lot at the coffeehouse and accompanied her in her car to her home.

Her husband was not there, and she invited me in for a drink and I accepted. I won't go into details of what then occurred, it being sufficient to say that the outcome was we made love in a very full and frank way, and it was an experience which totally overwhelmed me. Not only had I never experienced anything like it before but I'd never experienced lovemaking of any kind before, so I became completely enamored of her and found I could think of very little else at all times except her. It was also I suppose very flattering to me that a very beautiful woman such as she was should apparently reciprocate my feelings, and continue to do so. We met on many many occasions; we went to motels or out into the hills, and we met too at her home because her husband was away very often on business trips. I could only describe my attraction to her being one of complete obsession of an almost entirely physical or perhaps more correctly sexual nature.

She knew what my job was, and on one occasion she asked me in a casual fashion if I had access to a gun. When I said I didn't, not when I was off base and asked her why, she just laughed and it wasn't mentioned for a time. I actually thought nothing of it, but I should say that I was so enthralled by her that had she asked me could I get her an aircraft carrier I would probably have said I'd try.

This situation continued for three months or a little more, and then she told me one afternoon when we were in bed in her house that she'd been thinking very hard about the matter and was determined to tell her husband she no longer wished to be married to him and wanted them to be divorced. She asked me if I would marry her if that occurred and I said that I would of course. But what transpired was that when she did tell him he gave her a severe beating: she called me at the base and she was sobbing and crying and said she had left the house and was now at a motel and begged me to meet her there. When I went she took off all her clothes to show me how covered with bruises and marks from blows she was. Obviously he had hit her many times and very hard.

It's difficult for me to recall now so long afterwards what effect seeing her in that condition had on me. It made me angry of course, but I've come to realize that it must have caused me to react in a way which was even stronger than I supposed. It put me in a fury is perhaps the correct way to describe it. And just as making love to and being made love to by her had had the effect of arousing an erotic frenzy in me which had been far outside the parameters of what I'd ever previously experienced, so the anger produced by the sight of her badly beaten very beautiful body was also far beyond anything of its kind I'd ever felt before. I do remember saying to her "Wait here, I'm going to kill him" and then going out and getting into my car and leaving her at the motel.

For purposes of self-protection if it ever became necessary, I always carried a large hunting knife under the driving seat in my car, and I had this in my hand when I reached her home and went up the path and rang the bell. Although I'd never seen him face-to-face before, I knew the man who opened the door was her husband, and without saying anything I stepped forward and pushed the knife into his chest. He staggered backwards against the wall, and in doing so half turned away so that his back was in front of me, and I stabbed him there also. I think I described myself earlier to you as being in a state of frenzy: that this was so is borne out by the fact that I then continued to stab him a total of twenty or more times, even to the extent of being down over him when he'd fallen on the floor and continuing to thrust the knife into him. And just as I'm puzzled as to how I could begin and continue such a ferocious attack as I did, so equally I don't know why I stopped. I think it must have been due to emotional and physical exhaustion, at least that's how it now seems to me after considering it many times since it occurred. I did want to make absolutely sure he was dead too of course. At the time I didn't have any compunction about it: my only thought was that he had been so savage and cruel to Barbara, and for a long time afterwards I looked at it that way, persuading myself that what I'd done to him was only what he deserved. I think that was the bell.

The house wasn't very far from where someone else who worked on the base was living, so I decided to go there. My clothes were covered in blood and it was a warm summer's evening and light still. I must have walked past at least a dozen or twenty people in the street in that state, and to some of them it might have appeared I was injured and in need of help, but no one stopped me to ask, which in thinking about it I've often thought was strange. When I got to the house of the man I knew, he knew at once something serious had happened and asked me would I mind him taking me to the kitchen to wash, because they had visitors in their main room. I told him what had happened, that I'd killed someone, and asked him to call the police and ask them to come.

That bell that was ringing a few moments ago down the block in the corridor was the lunch bell, which means I should go to the canteen. May I come back afterwards and talk some more for a little while? Thank you.

I was taken to the police station and handed over to a group of detectives who took it in turns to write down my answers to their questions. There are a lot of stories about the police giving people a beating to force them to confess to something, but it wasn't in any way like that at all: they were all without exception very kind and understanding and didn't pressure or bully me in any way. I gave them a full confession, but I didn't want to involve Barbara in it so I told them I knew this man and had discovered he was having a love affair with my girlfriend and I said that was why I'd killed him. At no stage did I mention her name or give any details that could have identified her, and often when I've thought about it since it's always seemed strange to me they apparently accepted my story completely and didn't ask me more details than those I chose to give them.

Once or twice I became very tired and said I didn't want to talk anymore for a while; when I did that they always immediately let me have a break and took me back to the cell they were keeping me in. I asked for a cup of coffee or a cigarette occasionally and they always gave them to me. I was also at that time going through a phase of religious curiosity, by which I mean taking an interest in the subject which I'd never done before, so another thing I asked was could they lend me a Bible to read in my cell, which they very promptly produced for me. For several weeks I stayed at the police station and occasionally read it and thought about some of the things in it, but I didn't in any way undergo a dramatic conversion to religion or anything like that. At the time I had no religious belief and I remained in that state.

The police strongly advised me to contact an attorney: I didn't know of one so they kindly contacted one for me. When he came I said nothing to him except that I had made a number of statements admitting my guilt and they were all true. Like the police, he never asked me for any further details; he simply advised me to plead guilty and avoid a time-wasting trial. I took his advice, and no mention was ever made of Barbara or the true reason for the crime.

That was fifteen years ago now when I was twenty-three, and I've been in prison since that time. It was a particularly dreadful crime, and as I've thought about it over the years it's seemed to me that in summarizing it, I would say it resulted in three deaths. The first obviously was that of the man I killed. The second was the death of love, if love it was, for the woman concerned, because almost at the same moment I murdered her husband I seemed to be killing my love for her, and in a way freeing myself from it. I have never seen her or heard from her ever again, nor have I wanted to. And the third death was my own, because as I see it now I killed the spirit of God which was within me, albeit not very strongly at the time. Sometimes I've thought that it's almost as though I had to kill that before I could find a new faith to take its place.

This I did find after I'd been here about four years. What happened was that I began to feel that my nature, which you could describe as introspective, wasn't satisfactory for me to deal with the subject and sort out my feelings about it on my own, and I needed what might be called an input from outside. The idea of subjecting myself to psychiatry or psychotherapy has never greatly appealed to me, and as I had growing feelings about the importance of religion and God and the universe, I could be helped better by someone who might be like a spiritual adviser as it were.

So I wrote a short letter in identical words, saying that I needed help and advice in my search for faith. I sent one copy to the Protestant minister who serves this prison and one to the Catholic priest who does the same. I said I would like to talk to someone about possibly reestablishing my personal religious faith—that was the phrase I used. There are over fifteen hundred men in this prison and it's possible the Protestant minister never received the letter or was too busy to reply to it. I don't know what the reason was but I never had an answer from him. The Catholic priest came to see me the very next day, and he impressed me by not asking me what I'd done or anything about my crime, but merely talking to me as though I was an ordinary person who'd come into his church off the street to make a few inquiries about the Catholic faith in general terms. He gave me two short leaflets to read and said he'd come and see me again in a few days.

He was an elderly man with a very gruff manner: he said very little to me next time, and he didn't try to encourage me to join the Catholic Church. When I said I might be interested in it and in starting along that path, he told me crossly it couldn't be done like that, and said I'd have to do a good deal more thinking about it first. He continued to come and see me about once a week for several months and his attitude was always the same: he said he didn't think I was ready yet to believe. You could almost say he tried to discourage me, that was the impression he gave. He's either retired now or gone to a different parish, and although his successor was younger, his approach was the same kind of pragmatic and down-to-earth one. For a long time he was unwilling to talk about spiritual things, always saying everyone had to work everything out for himself in his own way.

In total it was five years before I was accepted into the church, and I've since found a lot of solace and comfort in it. On the majority of things on the whole I think the Catholic Church is pretty well right, though like many others who belong to it I've had a hard time thinking through its dogmas and beliefs to find out where I stand. One

example which has exercised me a lot is the idea of the Pope's infalli-
bility. I think he's quite right about abortion and that no one should
take the life of a fetus. Once conception's taken p'ace then life is
present and no one should terminate it. But I don'. think he's right
about it being wrong to prevent conception: I think if people don't
want to bring life into the world and prevent it happening by using
birth control of any kind they choose, then they've every right to
do that.

On the whole I always find Papal pronouncements very interesting, but in some respects I feel he ought to go further than he does
and denounce war totally, for example. Instead of making pious statements that he's praying for world peace, I think he should say quite
emphatically that all war is wrong and no Catholic should ever take
part in it. If abortion is sin because it's murder, then war is ten times
or a hundred times more sinful because it's mass murder. If he said
that loud and clear, the Pope would be making a much greater contri-
bution to peace than he does by just saying he's praying for it.

Two years ago we had another different Catholic priest appointed
here, and he asked me if I'd like to be his clerical assistant. I didn't
quite understand which way he meant me to take the word clerical at
first, but he meant in the writing sense: it's my task to keep his office
files in order, type letters for him and deal with his general correspondence. This has done a lot for me and made me feel that even in such
a very humble way I'm serving the Catholic Church. It's like a sort of
responsible PR job you might say, and if I do it properly there might
eventually be a chance of me taking a course of study in theology or
something of that sort. To be a priest would be a wonderful thing, but
obviously because of my crime there's no chance of that happening.
That doesn't mean there's any harm in me pretending about it
though; I sort of regard myself as someone who's practicing for the
priesthood. I get a great deal of enjoyment from doing it, because I'm
devoting my life to trying to be a good Catholic man, which you can
always do whatever your surroundings are.

I've no connections or foundations for any sort of physical or mental life outside of prison. I get two or three letters a year from my father or mother, but neither of them's ever visited me, nor have I heard in any way or at any time from my brother since I committed my crime. I did write to my father and mother asking them if they thought they might come and see me once, perhaps when they were taking their annual vacation. They live two thousand miles away and my mother replied that her father who is very old and ailing had to be their first priority—they always went to see him on their vacations. She said when he died they would see if they could work out a trip with an itinerary which would include coming here. That was six years ago and I presume the old man must still be alive because they haven't yet been. My other correspondence is from a Catholic pen friend in Montana, who writes once a year in response to an ad I put in a Catholic newspaper. She's a lady in her fifties and she sends me books occasionally. Most recently she's sent me a biography of the English Cardinal Newman which I found very interesting, and a translation of some poems by St. John of the Cross who's someone I hadn't heard of before. I don't know what she looks like and I intend to ask her for a photograph. From the way she writes I would imagine she's perhaps a schoolteacher or something, and she's certainly very kind.

Making a summation of my position, I would say that the thing I like most about the Catholic faith is its orderliness, and I've often thought if I were to be free I'd be happier not living in America but in a more orderly country such as England or Japan. I have a sense that they both have a more structured kind of society than ours, although I don't know very much about either of them. What little knowledge I have of England for example comes from reading such things as the spy stories of John le Carré, or its sense of humor as shown on television in something like *The Benny Hill Show,* which greatly appeals to me because of its quiet gentleness and its irony.

I accept totally the idea of imprisonment, either for the rest of my life or for some shorter period than that if that's what God decides. I see being here as a perfectly right and just punishment for the atrocious murder which I did, but I also see it as a way of life which suits me just as the Catholic Church does, namely that of existing in an institution subject to external discipline. At school I was always happy with the rules and regulations there, and again after that when I went in the navy I liked that because it was also an institution. And finally I came into prison, which is in many respects the ultimate physical form of it, just as the Catholic Church is its spiritual equivalent. Even my dream or fantasy as I should perhaps properly call it, of being a priest and living a life of obedience and celibacy contains all these same elements.

I could say and will say that I am very content here, and I don't find it difficult to remain aloof from most of the other prisoners. This isn't because I regard myself as in any way superior to them, which I don't: I think it's part of my nature to want to be separate from others and on my own. Only one thing is missing to make my situation ideally suited to me, which would be if I could have with me a dog as a companion—and he would be a dog like Ringle of course.

THE ROAD NOT
TAKEN

JOHN WHITMAN

Waiting in the empty interview room in the prison at eight o'clock in the morning, he was sitting on the edge of an unused desk, reading a book and swinging his bare legs. A tall thin man with gray hair, pale blue eyes and a lively voice, he wore shorts, sneakers, a Miami Dolphins T-shirt and a baseball cap.

Hi, no I've not been waiting long. Anyhow, I'm not going no place, I've plenty of time. This? *Mountain Interval,* poems by Robert Frost. You know his stuff? As far as poetry goes I guess I'd say he's my number one. My favorite's in here, "The Road Not Taken," I can recite it almost by heart.

> Two roads diverged in a wood, and I—
> I took the one less traveled by,
> And that has made all the difference.

That'd sum up my life story pretty good you could say. You know when he died, for me it was like losing a personal friend. I don't mean I knew him but his things'd always had a great effect on me, specially when I was a young man: they coincided with my own experiences and reactions like nothing else I ever read. Funny how some things strike you that way isn't it? Some music too. I often feel the same about Mozart: you hear something of his and whatever mood you're in at the moment he reflects it. It can be the same piece at different times too. One time you'll be sad yourself and it sounds sad, another time you'll hear it when your spirit's are up and it's lively and joyful, you'd not think it was the same piece. Heh hell, what d'you know: I never thought I'd be talking poetry and music this time of day, that's for sure.

Me and my background, well what shall I say? I'm fifty-three, I'm in my twenty-second year of imprisonment in this place which is what they call a second-level security facility: it's not max but it isn't open either. It's about as far as a lifer can get in the system until he's put on work release, that is if he ever is; but I don't think I'll ever be that, no siree.

As a convict with a sentence for second-degree murder I've no minimum time designated that I have to serve, and no maximum either. I could be here for the rest of my life and it looks like I probably shall be because I don't see how I'll ever get parole. I've made five applications so far and been up in front of the parole board each time but five times they've turned me down. The way I look at it is it's a kind of a class thing: we're both white middle class, them and me, and they won't let me out because I've let our class down.

While my parents were alive they were in there batting for me, particularly my dad. They said they'd take me back in their home, be responsible for me financially, guarantee I'd carry out whatever conditions and restrictions were applied, but he died ten years ago, and my ma a year after that, so there's kind of no one really on my side now at all. I don't have hopes, but being truthful with you I can't say freedom matters that much to me now. The length of time I've been incarcerated, I know if I was let out I wouldn't be able to cope with it, I'm completely institutionalized. Adjustment would be a real big problem and I don't think I could make it now, not at my age. I was thirty-one when I came in: that age you can start your life again, unlearn habits and handicaps, but I don't think you can at fifty-three. Only don't get me wrong, I'm not eating my heart out: what I've got now is what I'll settle for, I reckon it's as good as I'll ever get.

What might be called the basic social history of my life is perfectly ordinary. I didn't have a deprived childhood, I didn't come from a broken family, I was never into drugs and I had no previous convictions of any kind before this one. No unhappiness in my youth, no traumas, nothing—I was just an ordinary only child. I went to school, then to high school, and I graduated at seventeen. I wasn't much of a scholar, I liked music and reading but that's about all. My interest was in sport and particularly because of my height in basketball. I didn't have fancy ideas about being a pro though, nothing of that sort.

After graduation I had a chat with my dad about what to do, and he came up with the idea while I was young and without domestic obligations it might be good for me if I went in the military and maybe aimed for a short-term commission. That was okay by me so I went into the air force: I thought it might shake me up a little and mature me, give me time to think about the future and what would best suit me when I was more adult.

Two years into that I began to get things clarified: I decided I'd like to be a teacher and take advantage of one of the service training schemes on offer. They put you through college and you give them a kind of a half promise in return that when you're qualified you'll come back and teach at a service base school for two years. I ended up with a bachelor of arts degree, then I went to a base and I was there two years teaching English to the children of men in the air force. At that time I'd be around twenty-three: no no, you forget don't you, I was more like twenty-five.

I fell in love with another teacher at the base, a civilian girl who came in from outside, and when we'd been dating about six months we got married. She was twenty-one, very pretty, and a nice girl in every way: it looked like we'd do well together in life. Our respective parents approved and we had a big wedding with around two hundred guests. After that we both went on teaching, then three years later our daughter Sharon Yvonne was born.

I've never been able to think exactly why a year after that things started to go downhill, and fast. One important contributory factor was the Vietnam War which was on at the time; our views on it were diametrically opposed. Rosemary was totally against it, she was into demonstrations and protests and leafleting and all that, and I won't say I was fanatically in agreement with it, but I did have a sense of patriotism and the attitude I still have now, which is my country right or wrong. We had some real bitter arguments about it, and they didn't stop at agreeing to differ, a lot of bad feeling was aroused. She came from a traditional Republican family and I think she was reacting not only against me but her whole upbringing. My folks were Democrats but not radical; they weren't really that much interested in politics, and neither was I.

Then she met a man at some antiwar meeting or other and they began having a love affair. She didn't deceive me about it, she told me more or less from the start it was going on. For a while I held on hoping it'd blow over and thinking if they stopped seeing each other she and I could maybe begin again. One thing about it was we never fought: discussions on Vietnam would have us swearing at each other in two minutes flat, but open talk about her going off and spending a night with another guy never raised the temperature even one degree. Odd, but being from conventional backgrounds like we both were, we prided ourselves on being adult about things like that and talking them through in a civilized way.

Any signs of decrease in her enamoredness with this guy didn't show: it was more the reverse. It hurt me like hell inside but I didn't want her to know that, I felt it'd seem like emotional blackmail. The point came eventually though when she said she couldn't go on any longer with our marriage and wanted a divorce: she and her lover wanted to get married instead of going on as they were. After that our discussions centered on what would be the best for our daughter Sharon Yvonne. Both of us agreed that while she was as young as she was, it'd be better if she stayed with her mother. I made plain I wanted to contribute financially to her upbringing and we agreed on an amount; we considered every aspect of everything openly and left nothing unsaid or unresolved. I think we felt quite proud of ourselves.

Rosemary and I then went to El Paso in New Mexico and had a

twenty-four-hour divorce; she and her guy went to Texas after that, where her parents lived, and they took Sharon Yvonne. Subsequently, I never ever missed on my monthly payments for her, I called her up on the phone every week to talk with her, and everything went just as we'd agreed. I moved out of our apartment into a smaller one, and not long after that I changed my job. I moved up the academic ladder to be a college lecturer at a better salary, and under the end of that part of my life I quite consciously drew a line.

I'm not pretending it wasn't all traumatic for me, because it was. However good I'd behaved about it, I was hurt real deep inside. I'd loved Rosemary, she was the only woman I'd ever loved, and her going off with someone else was something I thought I'd never re- cover from; I don't know either to be frank about it that I ever did. On a basic level, when a woman tells her husband she likes being screwed by someone else better than she likes it with him, it strikes at the root of his manhood: it's probably the single most hurtful thing a woman can ever say. It left me completely desexed is the only way I can put it, and for more than four years afterwards I couldn't find it in me to have the slightest interest in looking for female company of any kind. I was frightened of being hurt again, but the lack of interest in sex was something much more: I wasn't deliberately holding myself back, my feelings were totally frozen out of existence. I thought they'd never come back ever, because after what'd happened I didn't believe they could.

I should have been aware though of what was happening inside me, I really should. I was all the time thinking of myself as incurably emotionally paralyzed, but of course what I was in reality was some- one walking around with his eyes shut tight, and getting nearer and nearer to the edge of a cliff. Because into my classroom for enrollment one day walked the most fantastically beautiful young girl I'd ever seen in my life, and as soon as I set eyes on her from that moment on I was totally lost.

She was ten years younger than me, she had olive skin and silky blond hair down to a tiny little waist, and a fantastic figure and long

long legs. She was partly Argentinian in origin and I learned later that women from there have the reputation of being the most beautiful women in the world. I think there's a lot in it. I fell hopelessly in love with her, and things happened so quick after that that even now I can't believe anything could ever go so fast. One day she came and enrolled, the next day I played tennis with her, and the third day we spent the entire day in bed. As quick as that. And among all the turmoil of emotions she set fire to in me, the one I felt above all was gratitude to her for bringing me back physically and sexually to life. I couldn't keep my hands off her, I wanted to kiss her and press her and stroke her and screw her like I'd never wanted to with anyone in the whole of my life before. I can only put it she made me feel if what I'd felt for Rosemary'd been love, what I felt for her to put it at its mildest was adoration yet something far far more. Her name was Consuela.

The idea of her being in my class and me trying to teach her and fifteen other students all at the same time was out of the question: I couldn't have concentrated and neither could she. We fixed it therefore for her to study under someone else. She moved straight into my apartment, and we were so wrapped up in each other we didn't care whether other people knew it or not. Both of us were unmarried, and her parents lived a couple of hundred miles away, so she told them she was sharing accommodation with another girl. It bolstered my ego enormously of course this beautiful young girl should be as physically passionate about me as I was about her, and I felt in every way I was like a newborn man. And thinking about her and what happened subsequently between us, this is the point where it goes like the Robert Frost poem: I took the road less traveled by and that was the one made all the difference. Within two weeks I'd asked her to marry me and she'd agreed. We found a judge to do it for us, we had a few days' honeymoon in Montana, and then we came back to college and moved into a brand-new bigger apartment.

Ella dropped out of college and got a job in the office of a construction company to bring some extra money in, and we spent God knows how many thousands of dollars on fittings and furnishings for the new home. And she was like a gorgeous doll: every new thing we got she squealed with delight about. She frowned and pouted with worry if she wasn't sure whether two colors went together, and she moved around touching and stroking everything and saying how beautiful it was that we should have our own home. Me, I just sat there with my heart fluttering, watching her and feeling sick all the time with physical desire.

Like in any marriage, you can't live for long in that sort of blissful enchantment and perpetual lovemaking: with us we'd shot up in the sky like a rocket, and equally quickly we fell back down. I started to learn things about Ella that in some ways I wished I hadn't known. The first was when she told me she'd had an abortion the year before because she hadn't wanted to have a child. From my angle that kind of prodded me into facing I wasn't her first man. It would have been ridiculous to expect anything different, but it aroused all my fears again about my sexual prowess: several times I was within a couple of seconds of bursting out with questions to her about it. What was he like, who was he, was he better at it than I am? No don't answer, don't tell me, I don't want to know; yes I do, tell me the truth, let's get it out in the open between us. It went on going round and round in my head.

Then I learned something else, that when she was eighteen she'd been hospitalized six months with a nervous breakdown. There's nothing to be ashamed of about having had mental illness, I know that, but once again—unreasonably I suppose—I felt it was something I wished I'd known earlier. There were other minor things too, like one of her brothers was a practicing homosexual, at fifteen she'd been fairly heavily into drugs, and things of that sort. What it all added up to was I started to realize something that'd been obvious from the beginning, namely that we didn't really know each other at all. I guess there must've been sides to me too she didn't learn about till we were married. I don't mean any of it made a difference to the way I felt about her—it didn't, only somehow it made me sort of apprehensive about what there might be to follow as it were. And I'm not saying if

I'd known more things I wouldn't have fallen for her the way I did, I'm sure I would have. What I think now is maybe what we should have had was a love affair to start with and a period of living together first rather than jumping into marriage so fast. But I was the older of the two of us, and it was me proposed to her, so there you go.

Things didn't go smoothly for us for less than a year, then it all declined into pretty well hell on wheels. I was a fairly placid character, but Ella wasn't, she was real volatile, and I felt I was struggling all the time to try and keep up and match all her different moods. One minute she'd be all gentle and calm and loving, then she'd make a quick switch and become a spitting fury and say she despised all men. After that she'd turn again and be a sex kitten sort of femme fatale who wanted to make love right there and then on the floor. I didn't know whether it was a typical situation of an older man and younger woman being tied to each other or a case of two individuals of opposite incompatible temperaments, or what.

Then after a year she became pregnant. I thought at the time that was a good thing, it'd calm things down and make our relationship more stable. I think at first she felt that way about it too, because there was no talk from her about not wanting a child. For quite a few weeks she seemed contented with it, almost maternal about the prospect. We discussed names we liked for boys and names we liked for girls and things like what sort of education we wanted it to have in the future when the child grew up. But Ella was that way only a short while, then she started fretting about where we lived was unsuitable, a second-floor apartment was going to be no place to have a baby in, and things of that sort.

Money wasn't a problem for us, so when she said the only proper surroundings to live in with a child would be a house and one that wasn't in the center of town, I told her to go ahead and see what she could find up to a certain price ceiling. That brought a big burst of affection and excitement from her in response: and every morning she got up earlier and earlier and took the car and drove what must have been hundreds of miles, scouring the whole area for what she thought would be the right place. Then she'd go in to work and resume the search again when she'd finished, and she'd not come home often till it was almost dark. She'd spread out notes and details and brochures all over the dining table, and we'd talk about the respective merits and demerits of houses till well after midnight every night as a rule.

Then she found one particular place she went crazy about. It was ten miles out of town and had some land around it, and in a lot of ways I imagine it was similar to an English country cottage in style, except it was built of wood. It stood on its own on a sort of grassed-over area by the side of a small lake with its own boathouse and landing dock and trees everywhere. It was as pretty as a picture and the first time I saw it was a sunny Sunday afternoon when she drove me out to look at it. I was as enamored with it as she was, and nothing else she looked at after it in any way compared. But the snag about it was a big one: the price of it was just around twenty thousand dollars more than we could afford. Ella always compared everything else she saw unfavorably with the house by the lake, and I did too; nowhere could come up to it in looks and character and setting. All that stood in the way was the price.

Once it gets to be like that in a situation, the outcome's pretty predictable I suppose. We borrowed money from my parents, and we borrowed more or less an equal amount from hers; with those sums and what we had in our savings plus what we could raise on a mortgage loan, that was it: we bought what we thought was going to be our dream home. I was determined things would work out in marriage this time around, and being fair about it I've got to say I'm pretty sure Ella made up her mind to settle down. I'm sure she meant it when she told me that she was the way she felt. Only if there was one thing Ella was, she was volatile: she couldn't help it, it was her basic nature every so often to quickly change. Two months later she went on a week's vacation to see her parents, and when she came back she told me she'd had an abortion. She said she'd thought things over and decided she was too young yet to have a child. I couldn't hardly believe what I was hearing when she said it; we'd never even discussed the subject before.

I didn't know what to do or say except keep on asking her why. There was something in her manner when she gave me answers that convinced me she was holding something back: she couldn't look me directly in the eye. Then finally she came out with what it was: she'd met a student who was her own age when she was at college, and for a long time since they'd been having an off-again on-again love affair, and she didn't want to have my child.

It was my second big failure with a marriage and it did, it got to me right in the depths of my soul. I couldn't work, I stayed home and drank for three days and the weekend, and the way it looked to me the only thing open for me to do was kill myself. I was eaten up with jealousy, I was at the bottom of the pit of depression, I was in utter despair. There was one very odd thing about it too: when Rosemary my first wife had given me the same message about loving someone else and not me, I'd put up a good front of being adult about it, and we'd sat down and talked. But when this same thing happened with Ella I was strangulated, I couldn't speak, I was literally struck dumb about it.

She went off to work Monday morning like everything was quite normal, and apparently she didn't have a worry in the world. It was a very hot summer and I spent the whole of the day sitting under a tree by the side of the lake staring at the water and drinking whiskey trying to numb my feelings. Finally I decided what I'd do, and when she came home that evening I told her what it was: I needed to go some place and get my mind straight, so I'd called my parents and was catching a plane to where they lived early the next afternoon. Ella just shrugged and said she thought maybe it was a good idea, and I asked her to come home at lunchtime with the car and drive me to the airport.

Next morning I packed my bag and hung around the house doing other things like calling the college and telling them I was sick and wouldn't be in till the following week. When lunchtime came Ella wasn't back so I started to get nervous because my plane was at two o'clock and there was only one flight a day. I called her at her office and said where was she; she said she'd been held up with something but she'd be home in half an hour. She wasn't, and I guess if I'd known she wasn't going to be, I'd have called a cab or something to make sure I caught the plane. But I didn't—another road not traveled, I suppose.

I'd always been a fairly pacific sort of a person and I'd never owned a gun. When we went to live in the house by the lake I'd bought a rifle because it was an isolated place and I felt it'd be wise to have some protection in case someone ever tried to break into the place. A few days after we'd moved in a neighbor offered me this gun so I bought it off him and kept it in a closet under the stairs. Ella didn't like the idea of it being there but I told her she might be glad of it one day.

By two o'clock she still wasn't home and it was obvious I wouldn't make the plane. I had a couple of whiskeys and then did what I often did when I was worried or upset at something: I sat at the piano and played. A couple of Beethoven piano pieces and some Schubert I think. What I also did, and there was no conscious reason for it I could ever think of since is I loaded the rifle and leaned it up against the side of the piano. It must sound strange to say I felt calm while I was playing the music, but I did, my head seemed like it was in another world. I don't think my intention was to kill her; I couldn't say what my intention was. I sat there playing and not thinking anything so far as I recall.

It was around a quarter after three when Ella finally arrived. I only became aware of it when I looked up and saw her standing in the doorway. I don't remember there being any expression on her face, not apologetic or ready for an argument or anything: she just stood there. I stopped playing and reached down and swung the gun around, then I stood up and went towards her. All I remember is she gave kind of a little shake of her head as though she couldn't believe it, and then I fired. It was a repeating type of rifle and I emptied six shots into her; I went on firing at her even after she'd dropped on the floor. Then I stepped over her body and went to the telephone and called the police: I gave them my name and address and said I'd shot my wife. Then I went out through the open sliding windows of the patio and walked down to the lake and sat under a tree and waited for them to come and fetch me.

Things went very badly for me at the trial. The area where we lived fancied itself as being rather classy, and this kind of thing nor anything like it had ever happened there before. It was like such a violent act sent a big shiver of horror through the whole community. The state prosecutor made great play with the fact I was a man of good education and intelligence, and I didn't need to have killed my wife. He hammered away at it that I could simply have parted from her like I'd done in my first marriage and come to an amicable agreement about it. I couldn't really argue about that, it was perfectly true what he said. The other thing that counted against me was that I'd loaded the gun and kept it by me at the piano, then perpetrated the murder in cold blood as it were. He said there was no reason for doing that, it was premeditation, and anyway there was another plane I could have caught the next day. These were all things I didn't have any answers for, and like there often is in these situations, there was all the time hanging in the air the suggestion the whole story wasn't coming out, it was me who was probably involved with someone else, not her. Before trial I'd been examined by three different psychiatrists, and none of them had been able to find any sign of mental abnormality in me, so I must have known what I was doing. The whole trial was against a background of wealthy and what you might call patrician families, and I must be some kind of deadly animal who'd somehow got among them.

The judge was a woman, and I think she must have felt things were so stacked against me I didn't have much chance. So to my and I think a lot of other people's surprise, she directed the jury not to bring in a verdict of guilty of first-degree murder, but of second-degree on the grounds of temporary mental disturbance. That was what they did; and it was that intervention of hers that saved my life.

I don't know what your system is in your country, but what we have here is the first time you come in front of the parole board, the relatives of the person you've killed also are there, and they say to the board how they feel about whether you should be released. Ella's parents really stuck the knife into me: they said I was older than she was, I'd set out from the beginning to get my hands on her money, the week she'd been home and spent with them she'd done nothing but cry and say how unhappy she was, she was frightened of me because I treated her brutally, I ran around with other women, I was known throughout the whole college as a Lothario, if I was ever let out they'd be in fear of their own lives because she'd told them I'd made threats against them, and in general for having slaughtered such a lovely innocent young girl I ought to have been given the death sentence anyway. What they said's still all in my record, and nothing I can say or do can change it or have any of it removed. I did once write them and ask if they'd reconsider some of it, but that was eight years ago and they've never replied. Each time I come up in front of the board now the hearing gets shorter and shorter: all they say every time is they're going to postpone a decision until the next time around.

I know what I did was wrong, and I don't know why I did it, except it must have been like the judge said, my mental balance was temporarily disturbed. I don't know why I didn't shoot myself instead of Ella, and I don't know why I shot her instead of breaking the marriage off in a civilized way. Saying it was because she made me miss my plane doesn't sound too good a reason for murdering her does it? The bottom line is Ella didn't like me which she had the perfect right not to, and wanted to be with some other man which she had a right to too. There's nothing she did makes her deserve to have been killed.

So here I am and here I stay. I don't have friends, I don't have visitors, I don't have correspondence from anyone and I don't have friends. Nothing happens and the days go by, the same today as tomorrow and the same again the next day. I don't even think about it anymore, I just accept that's how it is. It's only human nature to hope somehow things might change, and like everyone else in here I'm hoping some, and then some more. But not having faith; that I don't have any of at all. There's some other lines of Frost's I often think of:

> They cannot scare me with their empty spaces
> Between stars where no human race is.
> I have it in me so much nearer home.

They're appropriate for what I feel.

HAPPINESS IS JUST
A WORD

GUS WEBSTER

*A small bald-headed man with a yellowed lined face and lacklus-
ter eyes, he sat on a bench in the prison's deserted dining hall
talking in a strained hoarse voice, smoking cigarettes one after
another without pause, stubbing them out in an overflowing chipped
white saucer ashtray that he held in his hand.*

My name is Gus Webster and I'm sixty-nine. My crime was first-
degree felony murder. I was sentenced to death for it at the age of
twenty-four, but it was commuted to imprisonment for life. I've been
incarcerated so far now for just over forty-five years.

To give you some kind of background I'll summarize my life for
you as best I can, but all it amounts to really is one word, and that
word's institutions. I'm a product of them, I don't know any other
kind of life. As far back as I can remember I've been in one kind or
another of them since the day I was born.

I believe I'm the child of poor whites who lived in Tennessee. That
may or may not be true but it's what I've been told by social workers
over the years. Occasionally they came across bits of information
about me and passed them on. They say my father was an alcoholic
who never stayed in the same place very long, and my mother was a
schizophrenic who was confined to a mental hospital before I was
born. She had me while she was in there, then wandered off on her
own leaving me for someone else to look after. My last name, my
surname as it's called, may be hers or it may not, or it could be my

father's; which it is definitely I don't know. I'm told there was a patient registered with her name at that hospital, but nobody can find out much detail of how I appeared. She's obviously dead by now.

At birth I was passed on to an orphanage, and I grew up in state homes for children for my first sixteen years. They were like the permanent base, but there were occasional fosterings out for short periods at different stages. They were all only for short periods because I didn't stay with any of them for more than a few weeks at the most and then I ran away. I was picked up by the police when I was wandering the streets or out on country roads, and then returned by them to one of the orphanages I'd come from. My impression of foster parents is that every one of them were people doing it for payment rather than they had a liking for children. No one made any lasting impression on my memory—I couldn't even tell you one of their names. My recollection's of a whole series of different men or women in different homes, periods in a whole lot of orphanages, and taking lessons at any number of different schools. Between times I rode freight trains, hitchhiked on trucks and generally bummed around.

You know, it was a blur of faces all the time. They wasn't attached to persons, it was like they were all passing on a reel of film projected on a wall. I never had no kind of bond with any one of them at all. Even with a social worker or someone of that sort I had no lasting consistent relationship I recall: they always seemed to be changing. Not with anyone at all did I ever have what might be called an exchange of affection; I never knew what it meant and I still don't now. There was no one I ever felt warmth towards and no one came across either as displaying it to me. It wasn't mutual dislike, just nothing between me and anyone, nothing at all.

I've tried to write about how it felt in all of my childhood to be a cipher to people, no more than a name on a record sheet or a number on a file. I have this picture in my mind of the same thing happening every time: meeting someone in an office or somewhere and them pausing a minute before we started talking while they read up about me and checked out who I was. I came across the word *loner* in a magazine article not long ago: I looked it up in the dictionary to see how it was defined. It said a loner was a person with a preference for being independent and staying on his own. I was a loner all through my life, but it wasn't a matter of preference; I wasn't offered no choice, I never knew there was an alternative. Another word I looked up one time was "happiness": it said it was a state of having or giving great pleasure or joy. That's something I've not experienced either. For me happiness is just a word.

I've always had a feeling of not belonging anywhere, and I remember an instance that kind of confirmed it to me when I was thirteen or round about that age. I was placed in a state juvenile home in Nevada and one day a woman came who was a visiting social worker and she asked me into the office with her for us to have a talk. She said she'd been doing some digging around concerning me and she'd discovered the names and address of a couple in Tucson, Arizona, six hundred miles away who could possibly be related to me, maybe an uncle and aunt. She said would I like her to write them and perhaps enclose a letter from me also, asking if they'd correspond. I said sure I would, so she said okay she'd go ahead, but she warned me I shouldn't be too disappointed if we drew a blank. I wrote out a short letter for them along lines she dictated and gave it to her to send on.

The juvenile home was one which didn't have strict discipline or many rules and they didn't bother too much about locking things up. So in the evening I snuck back in the office when no one was there, and I took these people's address from the note she'd left in my file. I wanted to do more than just write them a letter, I wanted to meet with them and ask if they could tell me a little about my mother or father. Up till then I'd never come across one single person in my life who might be connected with them or could say they'd ever so much as seen them and what they looked like.

A couple of nights later I walked out from the orphanage and hitched my way into town. Then I took a long bus ride through the night and most of the day to Tucson. I slept in a derelict shack and next morning inquired of people back at the bus station where the address I had might be. Someone thought they knew it and told me it was a farm way out to the north. That involved me hitching another truck ride to find it and when I saw it at first it looked like a kind of wonderland. It was big and well kept up, and obviously the folks who lived there must have been pretty prosperous I thought. I walked up a long drive to the house and knocked on the door, and it was opened by a woman I remember was wearing a housecoat of some kind of blue velvet material which looked very smart.

I asked did the people whose name I had live there: she didn't tell me, and her reply was very sharp asking me why did I want to know? I didn't have no reason not to tell her; I said I was looking for them because I thought it could be they were relatives of mine. A look came on her face like it was set in concrete: she asked me was I the boy the social worker'd sent them a letter from they'd had the previous day. I said yes I was, and then she looked me straight in the face and said they didn't know me and they'd never heard of the people the social worker thought could have been my parents. I was going to say something in reply but before I could she said if I didn't get off their land immediately she was going to call the police.

I've often thought about it since and I don't have any feelings of bitterness towards the woman. I think she probably could have been correct. If homeless youths were all people who wanted to find themselves a good niche in life, her farm she had there would be a good target for anyone to aim at. She'd maybe had people before, arriving claiming to be some kind of long-lost relative. Anyway, I didn't say anything else to her, all I did was turn around and walk away.

After traveling all that way I didn't feel like going back to the state juvenile home in Nevada. Instead I made my way over to Georgia, doing casual work on farms and I lived rough then for around three years. I never stayed in any one place long, not because I was restless but because I developed a liking for the fact I could live how I liked, not eat meals or go to bed when somebody else said, and I could please myself about everything. But one day I was walking along the roadside some place where by the side of it there was an orchard of orange trees. The fruit on them was like no oranges I'd ever seen, big and juicy and tempting, so I went in the orchard because it had no fence or anything round it, and I plucked about six and set myself down to eat them on a slope by the road. After no more than five minutes a sheriff's car came by, and when he saw me he pulled his gun and stopped and came over and asked me what in hell I thought I was doing. I didn't react or anything to make him think I looked like I might be trouble: I only said I was hot and thirsty and the oranges looked good so I'd helped myself. He said that was enough for him, I was stealing. He made me get in the car and he drove us into town.

I couldn't understand why there was so much hassle about it; till then I'd never come up against the law. I was kept in a cell and the next day put in front of a court. I was charged with theft, wrongful entering of someone's property, vagrancy and I think other things too but I've forgotten just what. The end result was I was sentenced to two years in a juvenile correctional center, which I think was because they didn't know what else to do with me. I've no reason for saying it, only my suspicion is they contacted the state orphanage I'd been in, and they'd said I was too old for them or something, and they couldn't have me back.

So there I was, another period in an institution; but now it was for offenders and it was specifically a criminals' one. There were around sixteen hundred boys there. I didn't make any close friends with any of them but it was the first place I'd been where I got partly acquainted with other youngsters of my own age. I remember I listened to some of the stories some of them told about things they'd done and I was amazed: in comparison my own life had been very dull and uninteresting. I wasn't attracted to the idea of imitating them and living a life of crime, but it broadened my knowledge of what went on in the world: drugs, thieving, guns, knives, sex, pornography, homosexuality, prostitution and everything. It was a real education.

When I was set free I continued living my life the same way as I'd done previously. A description of what I was when I was twenty would be to say I was a bum, with a slight tendency towards petty thieving which I hadn't had before. I didn't do house burglaries or anything big—it went no further than taking something if it was lying around when nobody was looking and then selling it for what I could get. Pocket radios, watches from washrooms, wallets from coat pockets, all casual things of that sort. I also worked too if I had to: digging, cement mixing, nailing up boardwalks, car washing, all sorts. The only job of any real relevance is I worked a few months in a diner as a short-order cook.

There was another young guy there who was also a cook: he was an ex-con from California. It takes one to know one is a saying I've heard: there's definitely some truth in that. I don't know why it should be but if you've done time you can usually tell about somebody if they've done time too. You don't have to ask them or speak even, all you need do's look at them and watch the way they look back at you. Sometimes you might give a little nod to each other, to signify you know. It was like that with this guy from California, the first conversation we ever had when we were leaving one morning at the end of a shift wasn't "Have you ever been convicted?" it was "Where were you and how long did you do?"

One day we went out in the woods to shoot some wild turkey. I don't know where he'd got it but he had a gun, and I'd never handled one so he showed me how to. Before long our outings were on a regular basis once a week, and we started giving each other confidences about ourselves and telling each other our life stories. Mine was not very interesting, but he said he'd once actually pulled an armed robbery by breaking into someone's house. The next occasion we were out he mentioned he'd learned of a prospect and asked me how I'd feel about coming in on it: there'd be just the two of us, him and me. The idea scared me a little but I didn't want him to see that, so I said okay yes I would. We went back to town and had a drink on it and he told me what was in his mind.

He had information that there was a certain guy, a fairly small-time gambler who always had sums of cash in his house. They weren't big enough for him to start screaming about if he lost them, maybe not more than a thousand dollars or so at any one time, and he didn't take special security precautions, so it ought to be a pushover to go in and rob him. It was out of my class so far as anything I'd done before, but I thought about it and the excitement of it greatly appealed. Two nights or so later we set off in an automobile we'd taken from a parking lot, and we drove out to this house. Because of his record the guy I was with said if anything went wrong and we were caught, we'd get a lesser sentence if I was the one who went in and did the holdup: he'd stay outside in the car with the engine running ready for a quick getaway. He'd brought stockings with him for us to put over our heads, and I remember thinking this was what proper crime was about, and now I was heading for the big time.

I went up the steps at the front of the house and I did like you see in the movies, I banged on the door and I shouted "Open up! Police!" We'd figured a small-time gambler like him would be scared by that approach and not put up too much resistance, and when the door was opened quickly without questions it seemed to indicate we were right. A middle-aged woman answered the knock and straight away I jumped in the hallway with the gun and told her to back up. Another woman came out from one of the side rooms very scared with her hands up over her head. She asked who I was and what I wanted, and I said where was Alf or whatever the guy's name was. The first woman started to cry: she said he didn't live there, he lived in the house next door.

She was right: we'd come to the wrong address. I was standing in the hallway thinking obviously from the way she was behaving she was genuine and we'd made a mistake, and I was wondering how to get out. At that point all the lights in the hallway switched off and somebody jumped on my back from behind. I didn't see any details of him. Later I learned he was the same age as me and he was the younger woman's son. There was a struggle in the darkness. He was trying to get the gun from me and my feeling's always been the woman joined in too and tried to help him. Then suddenly the gun went off, just a single shot, and the guy slumped up against me and then slid down to the floor. The older one of the women must have found the light switch because the lights came on again, and there the guy was, lying dead with the side of his head blown in.

I had a real sick feeling inside of me; I knew I ought to be trying to run away, but I couldn't move. The younger one of the women looked like she was paralyzed too, but the old one reached out with her hand to the telephone and took it off the hook, and then after a minute said very quietly "Police." The three of us in our different ways were all in shock I guess; my memory just blacks out from there on, and I don't remember more. Me and the guy waiting in the car outside were both arrested and charged with felony murder. We were held for a year before we came for trial, and the outcome was the only one possible, we were both sentenced to go to the electric chair.

It was three years all told I was on death row waiting to be executed, and in that time I felt like I aged a hundred years. Nobody knew me or came to see me except my attorney; I was a sort of an unknown person to everyone, sitting there waiting week to week and from month to month. The attorney was what they call pro bono, he was paid for out of public funds, and I expect he thought my case was a lost cause. He said he'd contact the last juvenile home I'd been in but whether he did or not I don't know; nothing came back so far as I know in the way of a reply. It would have been ten years at least since I'd lived there: everyone who'd had any knowledge of me had moved away long since and my records had been lost or misplaced I suppose.

He didn't come to see me much, maybe once in three months but no more. All I recollect him saying to me was "Don't worry" and "It'll all come out good in the end" and other things like that. They didn't sound very convincing or inspiring and all round his enthusiasm wasn't very marked. If I was to say to you it was a lonely time that would be about it: but loneliness was something I'd always been used to, it'd been my constant companion the whole of my life and I didn't expect any different. After a year and a half I was told the news, I forget who by, that the other guy who'd been with me on the attempted robbery had been given a commutation to life imprisonment of his death sentence and it'd been on several grounds. One was he'd been outside in the car all the time and not even in the house when the shot was fired; another was his attorney had put up a persuasive argument that all the way along the line the idea had been wholly mine. Most important though and what finally swung it for him, so I understand, was he had family and they kept writing all the time to the state governor and asking him to show clemency.

There was no one to do the same for me or had any interest in doing it. All that could be said on my behalf was I'd had no genuine intention to kill anyone when I went in the house, and the gun had gone off by accident in a struggle in the dark with at least three people's hands on it. There'd been mine and the young man who was killed and very likely his mother's too, and no one could say for certain whose finger it was had been on the trigger when it went off. They weren't arguments with much conviction to them: someone had died, someone had to pay the price, and the only person who could do that was me.

There's a whole lot of formulations that are gone through in the way of appeals against sentence of death and a definite chronological order in which they're done. As far as I know my attorney went through them all in the right order, but none of them had a positive result. Dates for my execution were set and then postponed for the hearing of each appeal, but finally when they'd all run out the last date was fixed: it was for five minutes after midnight on the first Thursday of April in I think it was 1952. As the time got nearer and nearer I was so scared I didn't eat or speak, and I refused an offer for the chaplain to come and see me the night before I was due to die. I didn't have any religious belief and nothing was in me that aroused any desire to make a last minute conversion.

They came for me at nine-thirty on the Wednesday evening and moved me from my cell down into the execution chamber where I was to stay the last hours until the due time. It was very eerie because there were other people there such as guards and a doctor and prison officials, but none of them said anything at all to me or seemed to notice I was there. They were paying no attention to me, just kind of looking through me all the time. It was half an hour before midnight before anyone said anything to me: that was the prison warden who looked at me, then nodded at the chair and said "Time." They strapped my arms and legs in it and from behind me I could feel them putting a heavy metal cap on the top of my head and fixing some electric wires to connect with it. The warden then went off into a kind of separate chamber in front and to one side of me. It was his responsibility to pull the switch, and I could see him through the window of it, making a big show of concentrating on meters there and dials. I was numb; in my mind and my emotions I was dead already, and the only feeling I can remember is wishing they'd get on with it quickly and not wait for the hand of the clock on the wall to reach five after twelve.

In the room where the warden was was a telephone on a high desk. I couldn't hear that it rang but it must have, because the warden suddenly stopped what he was doing and went and lifted the receiver off the hook. He listened a few moments, then he nodded and put it back again. He looked at me through the glass window panel and he did a movement like this across with his hands in front of his face to signal it was off, then he came out back into the execution chamber and said "You've got a commutation." I closed my eyes and I completely blanked out unconscious.

When I opened my eyes I was in a hospital bed: I was under sedation and didn't know whether I was dead or what. My consciousness kept coming and going; I'd fall off into sleep, then half wake up again, then go back into unconsciousness once more. I was fed on liquids a day or so but gradually I began to sit up and eat a little. I remember taking some plain cookies at first and some milk. I was in the prison hospital where the nurses were all male, and one of them told me it was fifteen minutes before he was due to pull the switch that the warden had the telephone call. Nobody seemed to know why the sentence had been commuted to a life term, and it was about six months before I found out. Apparently the state governor had only heard at the last moment I was due to die that night, and he'd acted off the cuff but not given reasons. If he hadn't I wouldn't have been here today talking to you, so the fact I'm still alive is only due to his intercession on my behalf. I believe he was supposed to have later said something about me having been brought up from birth without parents or relatives and I was therefore everybody's responsibility in some kind of way: because I had no one to stand and plead for me, that wasn't sufficient reason for me to die. He was against the death penalty too I think. I wrote him a letter telling him as best as I was able my gratitude, and twenty years ago when he himself died I wrote his widow saying I owed my life to him and I'd always do the best with it I could. I guess she must have thought there weren't many available possibilities for that, but if she did I like to think I've proved her wrong. I went on from there determined I'd try and find a place somewhere in the scheme of things for a convicted murderer who'd been reprieved.

And I have: I've devoted my time over the years to starting and building up a scheme for kids, to inform them about crime and how they shouldn't ever start in on that kind of a way of life. At the beginning all I could do was write leaflets and short booklets for young people on the subject, but I've been doing it so many years now the whole thing's developed into something I think's one hundred percent worthwhile. The state authorities think so too, because now they back me on it every step of the way. They let me go out in the community on my own on honor leave: I go to schools if they invite me and give talks to their kids. In total so far I've been allowed out one hundred and sixty-six times; it's on my record and so's the fact that one hundred and sixty-six times I've come back here on my own. It isn't worth a wooden nickel though as far as me being given total freedom is concerned: I've applied eight times in the last ten years for a parole board hearing, and eight times I've been refused. I don't let my thoughts dwell too much on that, and I don't have any hopes the situation will change; after all I've nowhere to go and live but here. But I regard what I'm doing as important for the kids I go talk to, and also I like to think I'm proving a point to those who say murderers should be executed. My view is they shouldn't, because there are many ways they can make themselves of use to society. They can never bring back the person's life they took, but they can change themselves if someone gives them a chance to do it and then go on from there.

The way things are for me now is I'm incarcerated in my body here, but not in my mind. I couldn't go out that front gate any time I wanted, not without permission: if I did I'd be brought back and not let go on with what I do for the kids. But so long as I'm responsible in letting the authorities know in good time about speaking arrangements, tell them just exactly where I'm going and when and exactly when I'll be back, they don't put barriers in my way. They're straight with me, and I'm straight with them, and they know absolutely for sure that I won't ever let them down.

IV

SINGING THE BLUES

TWO IMPRISONED
WOMEN

SHE AND I

LESLEY ATWOOD

A short slim woman with sharply chiseled features and hazel eyes, her thick fair hair was chopped in a ragged fringe across her forehead. She wore a pink blouse and a black knee-length divided skirt, and a dangling chunky gold medallion on a chain round her neck. She sat outside in the fresh air on an old white metal seat, leaning her head back against the cell block wall, slowly winding a small embroidered handkerchief through her fingers while she talked.

Four months, that's all now, four months and I'll be out of here. I'll have been incarcerated then exactly seven years. Simply, I'd describe myself as an ordinary woman of twenty-nine who drew seven to ten and a half years for killing her husband who'd consistently mentally and physically abused her to the point where she couldn't take it anymore.

I'm of Polish descent originally; my grandparents came to America from Kraków a hundred years ago. My parents I'd say they are middle class: my dad has a sports goods store and my mother works for him as head cashier. They make a good living, and I'm the middle one of three girls. We never had a house because my mother won't live in one place too long; she never likes to have a place redecorated, she'd sooner move on somewhere else so it's always been a series of apartments we've had. My elder sister's married to a doctor and they have three kids: the youngest was married last year and I guess I'd say she's the one in the family I'm closest to—she's quite brainy, she's a food technologist. I'm sorry that's a jumble, my thoughts have been a lot that way lately. Maybe it's the prospect of being free. In here everything's routine, you know what's what exactly, there are no surprises so it's a disturbing idea.

I had a happy childhood and no great traumas or anything. My dad was always a great believer in education, especially for girls: he didn't think they should just be homemakers dependent on their husbands. In our homes there were always books and paintings, and he'd take us to art galleries and concerts whenever he had the chance. A high standard was expected of you at school and college all the time: if your grades weren't all they might be there wasn't disapproval exactly, but more a suggestion you weren't doing yourself justice, that was the attitude. I came out okay. At college I took a degree in child education and infant psychology and then I wanted to be a teacher in some area of that kind. That's what I would have done if I hadn't met the man I married. But when I did that I didn't give up the idea, I told myself I was just holding it in abeyance a while.

I was twenty-one and he was twenty-seven; his name was Ashley and I was knocked out by him when I met him the first time at the house of a friend. I guess I was a bit of a bluestocking, and he seemed to me very worldly and charming and attractive. I think lots of women found him the same. When I've looked back on it I've sometimes thought he and my friend were maybe having a love affair, but at the time such an idea never even crossed my mind. I don't know what it was about me that appealed to him and it really surprised me when he called me up a couple of days later and asked me to go out with him to a movie and a meal. Maybe it was something to do with the attraction of opposites. Before long we were dating regularly and I was very seriously in love.

He had his own apartment; he gave me the key to it and we spent nearly all our time together except when he was away. He was a salesman for a pharmaceuticals company and once every two weeks or so he'd be away a couple of nights. I think that kind of stoked up my feelings for him because I missed him so much when he was. What was unusual for a man only in his late twenties—he'd already been married three times. And it was something else which attracted me because he was completely open about it from day one. His explanations about the relationships and how all of them had ended in separation and divorce were very convincing and he told me them in a way that didn't make me feel he was asking for sympathy. Of course he was, he was doing just that: but he always talked about his lack of understanding of the right way to handle the problems involved, and he made jokey remarks which sounded as though he was putting himself down. His first marriage he said had gone wrong because he and his wife were too young: both of them only eighteen and first love for her and for him. Then it was only a few months before the ardor cooled and she went off with another guy. The second woman was much older than him and she was an incurable alcoholic and had to go into some place for treatment: she had therapy there and discovered she didn't think he was right for her so they agreed to divorce. The third one was schizophrenic and had had to be institutionalized.

He was very convincing with all his explaining. Like I say, the way he put it across made me feel life had given him a really raw deal, and it aroused very protective feelings in me for him. My parents didn't dislike him but they were reserved about welcoming him fully into the family circle: they were better judges of character than I was, but of course I couldn't see that at the time.

We'd met at the beginning of March, and he invited me to go to Cape Cod with him for the Easter weekend. To a conventional person like I was the idea was very romantic and exciting and when we were there he proposed to me in a very attractive way: he took me out for an evening stroll in the moonlight along the shore, and as we were walking along holding hands he said there was something he wanted to say. He said he knew I wouldn't believe it, but he found when we were together he was at peace with me in a way he'd been with no one else ever before. He said he knew he was no great catch for a clever well-educated person like me, but he felt he couldn't let the moment go by without telling me if I would marry him, he knew he would find himself and overcome his feelings of inadequacy and worthlessness that his three failed marriages had brought. It was an approach I guess a lot of women would find hard to resist, especially an inexperienced one who'd had a rather protected upbringing like I'd had.

I surprised myself though on the other hand by giving him the answer I did. I said I definitely loved him, only I wasn't sure we knew each other well enough; so I thought a good idea would be if we lived together a while first, to make sure it'd work out. I could never have imagined myself suggesting such a thing to a man, not considering my background. It's easy to be wise after the event, but I can see now despite how madly I was in love with him it must have been a reflection of some kind of doubt there was in my mind.

We went home after the weekend and had a talk with my dad. Ashley told him what'd happened: he'd proposed marriage but I felt I wasn't ready yet for a full commitment and we'd decided we'd live together for a few months as a start. My dad said if we did it'd upset my mother a lot because she wasn't too modern in her way of thinking. He wouldn't mind it himself but he thought we ought to think about her. The result was we did after all get married and I moved in with Ashley. This was thirteen weeks to the day after we'd met.

When things've gone wrong, you have to think as hard as you can why, and I suppose you think specially was it your fault? I've done a lot of that: inside of a prison you're thrown back on yourself so you don't have much else to do with your time. I can't say I've come up with any easy answers for why things went wrong. For the first year of our marriage I'd say on the whole it was mostly okay. Sex is obviously an early item to be considered: when you had a situation like we had, with him very experienced and me hardly at all, you naturally think about that as a likely fundamental cause of problems. But it wasn't so, I'm pretty sure of that: I can truly say for the first year as far as I can judge there were no problems in that area at all. Ashley never complained ever: he said he enjoyed teaching me, and I was a ready and willing pupil and had a lot of enjoyment from the lessons. If you're a person like I was, at the beginning you try everything you can to

please your man, and he'd say often it was better with me than he'd
ever known it before. In fact I'd go so far as to say sexual compatibility
lasted longer than anything else between us, it did.

We really didn't have quarrels about anything in the first year.
Missing each other when he went away and the pleasure we took in
each other when he came back from his trips—if anything that inten-
sified. We had no money problems either. He had a good wage and I
did supplementary work at a nearby school when I was asked to which
brought us some extra income: we had no need of it but it was good
for extras like going out weekends to high-priced restaurants and that
kind of thing. I'd have stopped working at once if he'd ever asked me
to, for any reason or for none at all, but whenever I queried him about
it he said it was good for me, it kept my mind alive. Another possibility I thought of was he might want us to start a family. I asked
him about it twice at least, and he gave me the same answer each time,
that we should postpone it a while and enjoy being on our own
together first.

The only suggestion he ever made of a change in our way of life, I
agreed with him straight away. He said often when he was on a trip he
felt lonesome, and how would I feel about going with him sometimes?
That pleased me, to think he felt that way: it had crossed my mind he
maybe took the chance to flirt a little with a lady client when he was
on his own, so to have him say he'd like it if I went along was a
reassuring thing. I started doing that, but only when he asked me to,
which soon came to mean for him every trip he made.

One other thing he specially liked doing on a Saturday or a Sunday in the evening was going to a disco, a good class one there was in a
nice part of town. They didn't allow just anyone in, only people who
dressed according to the rules, which were that casual clothes were
allowed but only when they were smart. Ashley's great ambition he
always joked about was to be a disc jockey, but as an amateur, and
they often let him have an hour's spot there on his own. He'd spend
hours working out what he was going to play and writing his links for
saying in between. In a club of that sort he'd have had lots of opportu-

nities if he'd wanted to to meet other women, but that was another thing he said he enjoyed more if I was there, so it got that I regularly accompanied him.

I've thought about this over and over, and as I see it now something was happening gradually that I didn't realize. Whether Ashley realized it either I couldn't say, but I don't imagine he did: it was a thing that took place slowly at first, and then it kind of grew. It was that after the first year Ashley more and more took me over, he occupied more and more of my personal individual space. I was happy to go along with it to begin with, and by the time I wanted to stop it was too late. Even if I was tired and feeling not so good because of my period perhaps, and I said I'd rather stay home a few days instead of going with him on his trips, the first time or two he'd say he couldn't manage without having me with him, then times after that he'd start being angry and say I was being selfish. He began to insist. If you feel somebody needs you that much, like I did, in the end you agree: in a way it makes you proud of yourself that someone should be so dependent on you. What you don't see is that in time it's the other way round: if it means to keep them in a good mood so you can stay happy yourself, then it's you who's dependent on them. Then it got to be the same way with the disco. If I'd been sleeping badly and didn't care for the idea of having to stay awake till two or three o'clock in the morning listening to loud music surrounded by cigarette smoke, it made no difference, I still had to go along.

Towards near the end of our second year of marriage I felt like I was becoming almost completely bogged down. We didn't go much to my parents and family because they still didn't care for him greatly and nor did he for them, and all my friends by then were only people who'd been his friends first and I'd met them through him. I was always having to put my own preferences and feelings aside and do whatever it was he wanted, and he was becoming a complete emotional and mental drain. We had sex when he wanted, not when I did. If I liked to watch some program or other on TV that was okay unless it crossed with something he wanted to see and then we had to watch that. He even chose when we should go to the movies, where we should eat, if I should cook a meal or if we'd go out. Every single thing was at first by Ashley's choice and then got to be at Ashley's command. We quarreled: to start with a little, then more, then a lot. Two new factors were entering into things as well: Ashley began drinking too much, and I went on drugs. Not hard drugs—I mean sedatives, tranquilizers, antidepressants. I took them in small quantities at the beginning, but soon I was on to larger and larger doses and taking them more often. My doctor, who of course had been picked out for me by Ashley, was the sort who reaches for his scrip pad the minute he sees you coming through the door.

And then a third and much worse factor came in: Ashley started to hit me. When we quarreled I was usually too zonked on pills to put up an argument or try and talk him out of something, I gave in usually and agreed with him early on. I don't think I changed from doing that, pills don't give you that kind of strength. Ashley at first didn't strike me with his fist clenched, it was no more than shoving me around; but more and more often if he was impatient with me not agreeing to do what he said, he'd hit me with the heel of his hand on my shoulder around here. And it quickly got worse and escalated into some real hard blows: not on my face where it would leave a mark that could be seen, but in my ribs or on my upper arms.

It stayed that way for another year at least, and one of the things that complicated the situation was he was always very contrite after it happened, he'd sit with his head in his hands crying and ask me to forgive him. I always did and he'd tell me to show I really had by kissing him and sitting on his knee and putting my arms round him and holding him. When I did, it then always aroused him and we'd go to bed and have sex to prove that we really did love each other in our hearts. Like I said, the sex was usually good even then: however much he'd just hurt me physically, I never pushed him away and refused and I never wanted to.

His temper grew shorter and shorter: in a period of six months he cracked two of my ribs, dislocated my elbow, and broke my collarbone. Each time when he realized what he'd done he'd put me in the car and rush me to the hospital to the casualty unit, and on the way he'd be desperately crying and begging me not to tell them how my injury'd been caused and say I'd had a fall. He swore he'd never hit me again ever anymore, so each time I'd do like he said. It wasn't because I was frightened of him but because I believed him, and I believed him because I wanted to, I guess. The tranqs or whatever I was on, they'd be another reason, but fundamentally I think I believed he did really love me and there was some kind of inner demon in him he couldn't control.

He ground me down into a very unlovely thing: I was a nobody, a no personality, someone who had no control over her life, who couldn't walk away or find even the faintest bit of dignity to protect herself with. I stayed home all day sleeping in a chair or lying on the sofa staring at TV, and often I couldn't make out what people were saying or what the picture was on the screen. All I did was wait for him to tell me what to do, whether to cook a meal or put on a smart dress and makeup and do my hair because we were going out. Whatever he said, I obeyed. Some nights he wanted to do nothing but stay home and drink—they were the worst ones of all. He'd unfasten the thick leather belt he had and tell me he'd beat me up with it unless I did certain things. Whether I did them or I didn't didn't make any difference; he always whipped me with it afterwards, then went blind drunk into the bedroom and fell on the bed asleep. The certain things he made me do, well I'd sooner not say.

He can only have been sick in his head, and it needed someone to tell him he ought to have treatment for it, otherwise there was no hope for me or for him. I wasn't the one who could: I hadn't the willpower to do anything but try and keep myself alive, and I was in a permanent state of mind-drugged misery, feeling nothing usually but how to stop both my physical and my mental pain. Then there came a Saturday night when instead of preparing himself to go to the disco, he called them up and said he was sick and couldn't come. After that he went to the drinks cupboard and began on a bottle of rum; half

way through it he went to the bedroom for his belt and then followed
what usually did. Sunday I had so many bruises and welts on my body
I couldn't hardly move and I slept all day in bed. I've a recollection of
him coming in sometime and getting in bed with me and saying he
was sorry and us having sex, but I don't know at what time it was. I
woke up around six in the evening: everything was quiet and I
thought maybe he'd gone out, so I got up and put on my bathrobe to
go make myself some coffee and take some more pills.

He was in an armchair with another bottle of rum on the floor
beside him, sitting watching a ball game on TV, but he'd gone to
sleep, his eyes were closed and he was snoring. I thought I'd make it to
the kitchen for the coffee and the pills, but I didn't, he woke up. He
had the belt in his hand and he started straight off lashing into me
with it without saying hardly one single word. I don't know why it
was, but that time it specially hurt: maybe it was I hadn't taken pills all
day, or what, I don't know. But I remember my whole body was so
sore from the night before I couldn't do anything but sob and yell and
screech with pain; and every few minutes he'd tip up the rum bottle
and take a gulp from it, then go on hitting me again. He was stagger-
ing and falling about everywhere, trying to reach and give me another
blow but nearly too drunk to stand. Finally he gave up on me though
and lurched off into the bedroom.

Again perhaps it was because I hadn't had my pills that day, but
suddenly my head came clear and a sort of resolve came into me I
thought I'd forgotten how to feel. I knew he kept a revolver in his
clothes bag he took with him when he went on trips, and I went to the
closet where the bag was and took it out. I'd never handled a gun
before, and it was much heavier than I thought—I needed both hands
to hold it. And like I was in a dream I walked slowly with it into the
bedroom. He was lying like always with his face down and snoring
with his arms spread out sideways. I felt very calm. I went to the side
of the bed and so I wouldn't miss I put the gun barrel against the side
of his head. When I pulled the trigger it was just like his skull shat-
tered and there was a big spurt of blood that came out all over my

robe. I turned around and walked out of the bedroom and went and sat in a chair. It was like I was suddenly overcome with exhaustion and couldn't stand.

I think I went to sleep. I guess I must have, because the next I remember was the place was full of police. My mom and dad were there: they told me later I'd called them and told them what I'd done, but I've no memory of that, only of feeling very tired. The police I remember as being kind. They didn't arrest me, they let me take a shower and pack up a suitcase, and my parents took me back with them to their home. I was bailed to my father but I never knew what the sum was, and I stayed at my parents' home until the trial came on four months afterwards. During that period my attorney fixed for me to have tests and examinations by different psychiatrists, and I also started in on treatment to wean me off all the drugs I'd been on. It was a hard time: I slept a lot and I cried a lot, I recall.

After my attorney'd had several discussions with the prosecutor and talked with me about them, I agreed to take a plea of guilty to second-degree murder with no defense of insanity. In return I'd be sentenced to between seven years minimum and a maximum of ten and a half. I've behaved myself all the time I've been in incarceration and not had a single infraction charge, so they're paroling me exactly when I've put in seven years which is June.

When I first came here I was very scared, like most people would be I guess of the unknown. From the movies and stories I'd read in magazines, my idea of prison was a place of roughness and violence and cruelty. As time went by it was a great relief to find it wasn't that way at all. Everyone was helpful: the staff were okay and the other prisoners were okay too. I discovered things in myself and about myself that were very positive in a lot of ways. After the first year when the authorities have had time to assess you and how you're going to behave, the mutual suspicion and tension in your relationship begins to fall away.

I worked in the library a while, then in the administration block on clerical work; after that I was given a job assisting in the center for kids, taking care of young children while their mothers were here on visits to their relatives or friends. I enjoy that; in a way it fits in with what I studied and trained for, and it's given me some practical experience for the future too. I'm beginning to start feeling I can become a creative person again and do something constructive. Another good aspect is that mixing with other prisoners has given me a better understanding of how women from all sorts of different backgrounds can become involved in crime. I've become much less judgmental about people we label as criminal, or I think I have. I've learned how it's not a simple matter of people being good or bad, or doing right or wrong, as them getting into situations they can't handle and it's often been not through any real fault of their own. They might have had deprived upbringings, or been involved with men, or been in desperate positions when they were trying to do what they thought was best for their kids: a lot of things like that, which eventually ended them up on the wrong side of the law.

I'd say my main learning experience of all though was how many other women there are like me, who've suffered physically and mentally at their husbands' or boyfriends' hands. Not all of them took the same way out as me, but several did, and there are a lot more in here besides who are here for some different reason but have experienced beatings and bruisings too. We have groups going all the time for pretty well everything—women who've been on drugs, or alcoholics, prostitutes, thieves—and you'll find hardly any of them hasn't got one member at least who's been the recipient of violence from a man some time. Maybe it's an exaggeration, but you get a feeling sometimes you can't get away from that there's a whole lot of women everywhere who think being brutalized by men is a normal part of life and it's almost as common an experience for a woman as having children. When you start going into the reasons why so many women accept it, you find the main one is the same as I had, clinging on to the hope if only they're nice enough to a man and obedient to him, one day he'll change. It seems like he never does, but for some reason or no reason at all, that's what we want to believe.

Hearing this same tune so often with all the same words has made me into someone who doesn't ever want to get into a relationship with a man which means any kind of physical contact at all. There's another woman here the same age as me, her name's Cheryl, and she and I've been working a lot together the last two years setting up a group where battered women can come together and talk. We meet for a couple of hours once a week and more than thirty people belong to it now. We don't exclude anyone who's got other problems: we tell our life stories and what violence we experienced and how we tried to handle it. Not one single woman who comes did successfully: in some cases we killed because we could see no other out, and in others people took drugs, or drank, or physically ran away. We've contacted various people on the outside and got together a whole raft of information about where a woman who's suffering from violence can turn to for help. One of the most useful-sounding ones we've just recently heard of is an organization called "My Sister's Place." It started in the Midwest I think—Chicago I believe. It was small at first but it's growing quickly as more people get to hear of it, and a lot of big cities have a local chapter now. It gives advice and support but they say one of the problems you have if you need to contact it is they're hard to find: they don't hand out their address and phone number too readily so they won't have men coming on to them looking for their wives, especially because by definition they'll be violent men.

This is a very positive thing I feel I've put my time to here. Cheryl was the one got things moving in the first place because she could see the need; now she and I are looking to find a couple of other women who'll keep it going after we leave. That'll be within a few weeks of each other, me June and her July.

Sometimes after a meeting she and I'll be talking over things people have said in the group: a woman will have told us her story and it's always one about pain. There's the pain she describes a man inflicted on her, and the pain she still has in talking about it and bringing it all back. And we look at each other and we say "Can you ever imagine two women together and one of them behaving like that?" I guess it might happen once maybe in a million times, someone somewhere'll be in that sort of relationship with someone else of her same sex. But women don't behave like that to each other, not that you seem to ever hear. They fight and scream and shout and maybe throw things a little, but one doesn't systematically beat the other one into a pulp.

What's gone on here for me personally too is something I never imagined could. Cheryl and I love each other and when we're out we're going to start a new life together. We love each other and we regard each other as partners and it'll take a lot now to break us up. It's common for there to be lesbian relationships between women in prison—there's not much alternative available in regard to sex—but I think even if we'd not been thrown together here and found we'd had experiences very alike with a man, if I'd met her outside when I was my own person and not in a drug mist I'd have been very attracted to her just the same. She's quiet, she's sensitive, she's understanding and each of us can sometimes make the other one laugh. The most important thing though I guess is we've built up each other's confidence again; we can feel love, we can say tender loving things to each other without being scared of being vulnerable and hurt. What matters in any relationship is trust between you and being easy with each other when you're together: that's something we've both had to learn again from the beginning how to do. Some people might not believe two women can have a relationship as good and close as ours, and some people might think it can't be true and valid because of the difference in the color of our skins, she's black and I'm white. But as far as Cheryl's concerned and I'm concerned we don't even notice that anymore: we're one and the same person, she and I.

I MIGHT MAKE
ANOTHER LEMON

VIRGINIA HAMILTON

*I*n the late afternoon the long high-ceilinged visiting room was
*empty, its lights switched off and a few last beams of sunlight
coming in through the barred windows and playing on the rows of
deserted tables and unoccupied chairs. Near the entrance a bored super-
vising guard sat under a wall light at a lectern, idly turning the pages of a
newspaper and biting her nails. Far away at the other end of the room a
small plump figure wearing kitchen overalls and shabby white pumps got
to her feet nervously and tentatively waved her hand. Middle-aged, black
and stockily built, she blew her nose vigorously and wiped away tears.*

Gosh I'm sorry it's been the waiting's got me all screwed up inside. I don't have many folk come to see me, but I'll be okay now: yes
sure I will, sure.

Well then now, my name is Virginia Anne Hamilton. I'm a forty-
eight-year-old black lady and I have three children and three grandchildren, and I've been in here seventeen years. I'm serving a life
sentence for the murder by shooting of my husband, which I did when
I had passed just thirty-one years of age.

My mother died giving birth to me, and my father remarried
when I was four. Till that time I'd been the only one, but then he and
my stepmother had four more children together, two of them boys
and two of them girls. I remember how when I was a young person,
you know like a girl growing into my teens, I didn't get along too well
with my stepmother in those early days. When they were little her

children teased me she was their mother but not really mine. They made that difference, but she didn't though; she was good to me and when I grew up we got to be real close so that was okay. She still is close, too: my father's dead but all through the years she's always been my friend.

One thing didn't help the situation much with my brothers and sisters when I was a child was something I've not realized till I was grown. It was I was my father's favorite all the way. They were jealous of that because he spoiled me rotten, and I was envious of them if he gave them attention, so there was always a strain. That was as kids though; now it's all gone. We talk about it when they come to see me once a year, even have a laugh about it too. I don't think any of us were real unhappy about it, not really, you know?

In the family background we had, we were kind of insulated in a way. We were a black family with a nice house and a good standard of living: this was in a longtime mixed area in Boston and we never had no trouble with neighbors or anything. But what did cut us off from our neighbors was we were a very religious family, I think that was the cause. Sunday was never for socializing, it was always for church. There was Sunday school at nine-thirty in the morning followed by worship, church family hour after that, and Bible fellowship in the afternoon. Sunday night it was church again, so the whole day was taken up with it from when we got up till its end. To me it wasn't oppressive or anything, though, I was pleased to go along with it. So I'd say all together I had a good solid Christian background all the time I was a child.

I liked school and mostly did okay: I'd not claim I was the most brilliant of scholars, and I'd no great aim in view for my future. I liked reading most: love books, historical romances, only nothing you could say was great literature I suppose. My ambition was to be a mother with children, have a nice guy for a husband and make a happy family life like I'd had myself. An ordinary girl, that's what I'd say: not pretty, not ugly, and not one that would be called a street girl because my parents were careful never to let me stray. There was always a fixed time for me to be at home at nights, going up a little each year with my age. They were strict about who I played with when I was young, and stricter still when I was at high school about who I dated there.

It was there I had my only boyfriend and he became my husband in the end. He was a pupil one class higher than me, and his name was John; I never dated anyone else besides him ever at all, we were childhood sweethearts and that's how it stayed. My parents liked him too, but my stepmother did say to me once couldn't I find a nice colored boy? She only said it just that one time though, and after that it was never mentioned, never at all. Everything was always very strict and proper too. One occasion when there was the high school prom my parents drove me to the school and handed me into John's care at the door, then they came back for me at the end of the evening again and took me home. That was my entire experience of dating when I was a girl.

When I was eighteen and graduated from school I went on to college and took general studies a while. It was what you might say was a preliminary before I decided my definite aim. History and literature I was okay with, but darned near hopeless with everything else. My stepmother was very disappointed when I flunked math: she said it was essential to have it for most every kind of job. She had ideas I should work in a bank or a solid financial institution of that kind. That was always regarded as sensible for a girl.

My thoughts weren't really on it, on education I mean. Being away at college meant I didn't see John often. After high school he went to work with his father as a trainee insurance salesman, and the only times we had together was weekends if I was home. When I reached twenty he was on a good income and I felt very low: the way I saw it he was out making his way in the world while me, I was still only at school. I was sure it couldn't be long before he met another girl who was prettier and cleverer than I was and then I'd lose him.

Then I went home one weekend and saw him and he told me he missed me the same way I did him. Oh I was so excited, I couldn't believe it was possible he should feel like that. He asked me if I'd marry him when I'd finished my college course and I said I'd marry him right away and college could go hang. We both went and talked to our parents and they all seemed happy for us, so we married and found an apartment and started our first home.

For our honeymoon we went to Canada, and can you imagine what? The trip was our wedding present from my father and step-mother, the rental of a log cabin for two weeks in the woods by a lake. A big log cabin, a luxury one, it had sleeping accommodation for eight. So the family all came with us for all of the time; my father and mother and their four children, and me and John. We got along fine and it was good, even if it wasn't exactly how most folk would think of a honeymoon. Somehow it didn't worry us though, in no way at all. We didn't think it was unusual or peculiar, it was as though we were all one big happy family, and I suppose we were.

We had three children, John and I in the next few years: the first was born a year to the day after our wedding, the second a year after, and the third in about a further eighteen months' time. Two girls and a boy we had, and I stayed home to look after them, and John worked hard to provide. He was a good husband and a good father always. When he was home he did all the things a father should, like changing diapers, getting up in the night if one of them cried, taking us as a family to the park or a picnic at the lakeside. He couldn't be faulted, not in any way there was.

Like I told you, we'd been childhood sweethearts and so far as I know neither of us had ever had another partner in a sexual relation-ship as it might be called. Neither of us was very experienced or exciting, but for me I thought that was probably how most people's marriages were so it didn't bother me much. Maybe it should have, because after five years there wasn't much going between us, not on the physical side. I'd never any reason to think while he was away John had other women, and I certainly never contemplated any other man. John did begin to drink though, more than a little when he was home. One night when I woke up and found he wasn't in our bed I got up to look for him and he was sitting drinking by himself in the kitchen and looking unhappy, and when I asked him the reason he started to cry.

He said something seemed to have gone out of our life together:

he didn't know what it was, and he didn't know why. He asked me was I happy with him, and I said I was, which was true, but when I asked him the same question in reverse, was he happy with me, he said to be honest he wasn't sure. We'd known each other from when we were at high school together and it'd always been that we could talk. So we decided we'd be adult about it and see if we could get help; it took us a few weeks before we found one we both liked but then we began regular sessions with a counselor.

They say talking things through together with a qualified person can help you when you're in marital stress. Maybe it does for some persons, but for us it didn't, it made things much worse. I'm not saying I wasn't at fault in this, but John would get very angry after each session when we got home and shout at me for what he called giving confidences to a stranger. I said I thought that was the basic idea of it, that we should both honestly say what our feelings were, but he'd quote back at me words I'd used and say I was trying to get the counselor on my side. Things got real bad after a time because I was scared of saying the wrong things: so this was another problem for us and one which we talked through again and decided we'd make a change. I guess we were trying all the time to handle things the right way, but it never came out like that, always it all went wrong.

The counselor was a black man and he agreed it might be a good idea like we'd decided, that each of us had separate sessions with him on our own. But after a couple of times of that John said he wasn't happy with it and he wanted to see a different person to the one I saw and he'd like to talk on his own with a white man. I'd never heard him say anything of that kind before, I mean referring to the difference in our color, and I thought maybe the black counselor might take it he was racially prejudiced. But if he did he didn't show it, and the week after that John began having his sessions with a white counselor.

Only again it went wrong. Though he'd been the one who'd suggested we should be separate in our talks, only a couple more weeks went by and then John started complaining again. He accused me of being in love with my counselor and maneuvering things so's I could be with him on my own. I was getting desperate by then; I told him okay I'd have a new counselor and he could pick one for me black, white, male, or female, I didn't mind. Two days or so after that John said he thought the whole idea of going to counselors was a real bad one, which it was by then, I couldn't argue otherwise. So we gave up on talking through our problems or trying to, and it'd all been very unsettling for both of us in the end.

The next way we tried of handling it was we decided we'd move to a new home. We'd been too close to both of our parents we thought, and if we went some place else that was further away we could start a new life entirely of our own. It took us only a month to find some-where: it was no great mansion in a place of scenic glory, just an ordinary house on an ordinary street in a quiet good neighborhood on the outskirts of town. It was modern and clapboard, and freshly painted gray and white, and with a lawn at the front and a good-sized backyard. Also it had three bedrooms, which was good because our son was eight by then and he could have a room of his own. We fixed up the kids' schooling, and I think both of us thought we were set. Not set to be happy like someone had waved a magic wand, but ready to start in on rebuilding our marriage again.

Sometimes you look along your street, and you wonder how many other people there are, your neighbors and living in a house like yours, who are the same kind of situation too; you know, putting a front up in face of the world. Ordinary everyday middle-class Amer-ica: you wonder if it's got happiness, or whether things aren't going on inside those houses that aren't ordinary at all. There's no way of telling, because people don't talk about it except in places like prisons. They do there though, and they all say the same thing which is how unhappy they were.

I don't know how you start rebuilding a marriage, but whatever the way to do it is, it isn't the one that we tried. Materially we had everything: two cars, the house with a TV set in every room, plug-in telephones, two shower rooms, a new kitchen with all the gadgetry, everything. All we didn't have was have much social life: John was away traveling all week and when he was home he didn't care to go out driving anymore in the car. I hardly knew any of my neighbors which I see now wasn't a good thing. I'd meals to get at the end of the day when the kids were home from school, they had their friends in a lot, and I'd say mostly it wasn't too bad and I did okay. The one thing the bottom did seem it had dropped out of though was John's and my relationship: we never hardly spoke to each other ever at all. We kind of grated on each other, the smallest thing started a quarrel between us, so after a while we both felt it was better not to talk.

Oh look it's gone five. I'm sorry I have to go now or I'll miss my evening food. If you'll excuse me I'll be back again here in one hour. I thought it might be difficult for me talking, but it's not been, it's been easier than I thought.

Can I smoke, will it trouble you? Okay, if you're sure.

I guess now I ought to tell you this is the point where from here on in all the troubles we had, or leastways most of them, are down to me. I was a young married woman who should have been contented with what she had, which was three lovely children and a good comfortable home. But I wasn't, or for not very long, because then like you read in all the romance books, fate or whatever you want to call it took a hand. I'd taken the kids to school one morning like always, then I came home for a cup of coffee before going out to the shopping mall. I'd left the car outside in the driveway, and when I came to try and start it again I couldn't, I don't know why. I had the hood up while I was looking in the engine to see if I could find what was wrong, and a man passing on the sidewalk stopped and asked me could he help? He soon had it fixed for me and I thought well the least I could do in return was ask him in for a cup of coffee. We sat for a while in the kitchen and got acquainted with each other a little.

He lived just across the street five or six houses further on, and he said he'd moved in a month or so earlier. He was white, he lived on his own, he didn't go out much and him and his wife had just gotten divorced. He showed me pictures of his kids and I liked him, I was attracted to him, he seemed a quiet sensitive sort of a guy. That was it that day, that was all, and when John came home at the weekend it wasn't important enough to even mention it to him, leastways that's what I thought. But you're never sure how things are developing inside of you, or you're not at the time. One day the next week I was going to fetch the kids from school and just as I was getting in my car, David came by. We had a few words together about nothing, and then one day the week after that he came over and asked could he borrow a hammer or something, he was putting new carpet down in his home. In not long I was thinking up little excuses for going over to see him on some pretext or other, and later he told me that at that same time he was doing the same. What happened was inevitable—we were madly in love with each other before very long.

He was a part-time college lecturer and this being a time he wanted to get his new house in order, most days he was home. I was a very moral-minded woman or I'd always been till then, and I could never have imagined myself coming to behave the way I did, not ever before in my life. But I became his lover and for a few weeks we had a very happy and passionate time and thought of nothing and no one else at all. My ideas about propriety went out the window: times I wasn't with him were unbearable for me and he was the person I wanted to be with every minute of the day. Each morning I'd take the kids to school, then come straight back home and go over to his place, or he'd come to mine. I was crazy for him: I'd known love when I was younger and with John, but this thing between me and David was in a different league. Naturally I told him about my unhappiness, and he consoled me of course. We talked of me leaving John and taking the children, and David said he's support them and he meant it, I'm sure.

We were careful; the kids didn't know he existed nor that anything was going on. I was never in his house when they came home from school, and he was never in mine. But we weren't as careful as we should have been; though the kids never suspected anything, John did. I realize now but I didn't then because maybe I was suddenly happy around the place, or I don't know what. I think a woman's husband always knows or guesses somehow when his wife's having an affair; she takes baths more often or puts her makeup on with special care or hums or things like that. I know I shouldn't have cheated on him though; I should have told him straight out how it was. You do tell yourself that's what you'll do, only you won't spoil your happiness a while, you'll tell him tomorrow or next week. And because I procrastinated about it like that, I left it too late and I missed my chance. One morning I'd been over at David's and when I got back home John's car was there, setting in our drive. He'd had a cancellation of two appointments, which had given him a day with nothing to do so he'd come home. I guess he didn't have to be too clever when I walked in wearing my perfume and my pretty clothes to realize I hadn't just been out for a shopping trip, it was something more.

I'd never seen John in a rage and I've never been good at hiding things so he had me telling him the truth in five minutes or less. Yes there was another man I said, but I didn't tell him who or where, and I asked him could we talk it through like we had done our marriage problems before. I tried to stay calm about it, but I was sick to my stomach inside. He was way beyond reason, he shouted and raved. He said I was colored trash, I was a cheat and a whore. I was his wife and I belonged to him, I was his property almost and no other man was going to have me. He beat me and slapped me and kicked me, and he said he was going to make his point in a way I'd never forget, and he raped me right there on the floor. Then he left the house and got in his car and drove off I don't know where.

I could hardly stand. I had a bath and put fresh clothes on and then I went over to David's house but he wasn't there—I think he'd had to go to the college and take a seminar. I was terrified John would come back again and find me, so I took my car and drove into town to the police station where I made a complaint about what he'd done. Maybe I was unlucky there, I don't really know, but the white officer I told my story to treated it in a very offhand way, and a couple of times he shook his head and smiled. When I'd done he said I'd no grounds for complaint: if it was true John was my husband I had obligations to him, he could do what he liked with me and I'd have no redress because the law couldn't interfere. It was past time by then for me to go get the children, so I drove to the school for them and took them home. I'm sure they could see I'd been crying and maybe my face was bruised, but nothing was said, and when we got to the house John was there again. While they were eating their meal he came into the kitchen and said I must go, he couldn't stand to have me there. So I went and packed a bag with a few night things for myself and left in my car. The kids were watching TV and I didn't say good-bye.

I was in no kind of a mental state to think what I was doing, and what I did then was so stupid you wouldn't believe. I stopped the car outside David's house and went to his door and rang the bell to see if he was home. He wasn't and I drove off again, but I didn't have the sense to think John would be watching and see where I'd gone first. I went to a motel in town and spent the night there on my own. I called David up and we had a talk, and he said I should go to his house the next morning and we'd take it from there. I called up John too and told him I wasn't ever coming home, but I wanted to talk to him about a divorce. He sounded less angry by then, I thought he sounded like he was reasonable and calm. So I fixed with him I'd be at our house at eleven the following morning while the children were at school.

First I called at David's house, like we'd arranged. He didn't want me to go over to John's, least not without him to look after me, but I told him I could handle it and I wouldn't argue with John or anything; if he got in a fit again I'd straight away leave. David said okay then, but I must promise him to take something with me for protection, and he gave me a gun. It was a repeater, a small revolver, and he showed me how it worked. I hadn't handled one ever before, and in my mind I told myself there were no circumstances in which I'd use it: I'd keep it in my purse and only take it out and threaten John with it when I went over to talk if he looked like he was going to attack me again and I couldn't get away. Then David had to go off to college for a meeting of the staff but he promised he'd be back by noon and he said if I wasn't there he'd come straight over to my home for me.

It was around ten when he took off, and I made myself some

coffee and took a sedative pill so that by the time I saw John I'd be calm and in control. But I still wasn't thinking straight—the idea of what might happen, it just never entered my mind. It was only five minutes after David had gone there was a ring at the door, and when I answered it John was standing outside. He'd been watching till he saw David go, but he knew I was there because my car was setting at the curb.

He was smiling and pleasant, nothing about him made me think there was any reason at all for me to be afraid. He said rather than wait for me he'd come on over for our talk. I think when you're in someone else's house you don't expect another person to start anything, so I asked him in and took him back to the kitchen where the coffee was I'd made. But then well, only five minutes after it was like I never could have imagined. It didn't seem to make no difference to John where we were, he started in again very quickly building himself up for another rage. He got long past the stage where I could even begin to try and talk him down; he wouldn't let me say one complete sentence, he went on just like he'd done the day before, shouting and swearing and calling me names. And me, I was afraid the same thing would happen again; in fact I was sure it would, so I went to my purse on the sink top and took out the gun and told him to leave.

I couldn't believe what I was doing and neither did John: all he did was laugh at me mockingly and say I wouldn't dare. He was still laughing at me as he was coming towards me with his hand stretched out to take the gun, so I fired. It's still all very clear to me, it's still always easy for me to see it all in my mind. The bullet hit him right here plumb in the middle of his chest, but he just stopped and stood there and smiled. I didn't know anything about firearms, I thought one shot wasn't enough maybe, so I pulled the trigger again and again, and all of the bullets went one by one right into his body till he fell on the floor. After that I'm not sure what I did, it gets to be a blur. I think I just set in a chair and waited till David got back. I forget, I'm not sure.

This isn't a good story to tell, I know that, and it wasn't one that went down good any way in court. I was a married woman having a love affair; I shot my husband not once but six times; he was white and I was black; and at no time afterwards did I express any remorse. I couldn't, because something happened that destroyed me in the six months I was in custody while I was waiting my trial. It was that David caught some virus infection which turned to pneumonia and he died. After that I didn't care, not for anything or anyone—not for myself and not for my kids then even, I'm sorry to say.

My parents took them to live with them, and they did, they brought them up fine. They all come to see me now. I don't know how, but all of them seem like they've forgiven me, though it was their father I killed. I think that's more than most kids would have, but they're all three married and doing well. The eldest is my daughter Arlene, she has two children; the next one Bea has one; and the youngest who's my son Lance he's no children yet. But they write, they come and see me and they bring me my grandchildren to see, a long journey though it is that all of them have. I'd say I'm a very fortunate woman, and when I'm out, if that ever happens, they've promised they'll take care of me and see I've a home. I think maybe if I was free I'd marry again then they wouldn't have the responsibility for me, but sometimes I think I never will. It's too much of a chance to take. I might make another lemon, who can tell? Prison doesn't prepare you for relationships too well.

How long I'll do still, well that I don't know. My sentence was life and up till now it's been seventeen years. I'd like to try and better myself while I'm here, but there's not that many programs to choose from if you're a woman as there are for men. Mostly I read and mind my own business. I read love books and write letters to my family and talk with women my own age. I don't feel close to the young ones, but I play tapes my kids send in for me now and again. I've five times applied for a parole hearing, only till now I've not yet once been seen by the board. One of the problems here is the state governor: he was elected a second term a while back, and his line's always been that he's tough on crime: so I don't give myself a lot of hopes, not really, not while he's around.

I hope I've not sounded to you too sorry for myself. If David was alive I might feel different, but he's not so I don't greatly care what becomes of me: I don't feel it matters too much really, not to anyone at all. There's a lot of women in here like that and who've had unluckier lives. One way or another you know, we're all of us singing the blues.

V

THE VIOLENCE OF OUR LIVES

FOUR MEN IN PRISON

FEELING BAD ABOUT THURSDAYS

VINCE VICARIO

*O*ne of a trio on a small raised platform in a Sunday evening concert for a group of visitors, he looked concentratedly down at his deft fingers as he played his acoustic guitar and sang his softly gentle song.

> Oh let me say
> That all I want is you . . .
> It's all I do
> And I'll always be true
> To no one but you
> In my heart for ever
> For ever and ever. . . .

A slightly built man with neatly trimmed black hair and a swarthy complexion, he let the last chord slowly die away and then inclined his head modestly with a smile to acknowledge the applause.

Thanks, I'm glad you liked it—most people seem to, it's one of my newest ones. There's tunes all the time in my head; I practice them to myself and try them out on some of the guys. If they like one I add it to my repertoire and do it the next time we put on a little show like today. I can't write music so I have to keep songs in my brain. Oh no, there's no one they're written for except me: I just let the words follow the notes or the notes follow the words. It's something to do that's all,

161

something to do with my life, let's put it that way. There's sure not much else to do with it, not with my sentence: it's two terms consecutive of ninety-nine years each with no parole. I worked it out, it totals one hundred and ninety-eight years. So far I've got in around twenty I think, so that's only one hundred and fifty-eight more or somewhere around that for me to do.

Who I am, what I am. Sure okay well let me tell you. My name's Vincent Vicario only my friends call me Vince, I'm thirty-six years of age, and I'll be incarcerated the rest of my life or maybe longer if they can find some method of preserving a corpse. I'm not too downhearted about it. Some folk might see it I have a certain lack of prospects, but in fact there's times I get a little lightheaded pleasure at the thought that I'll never no more have to file a tax return, or worry about where I'll spend my vacation, or any shit like that. I can lead my life exactly like I want to, so long as what I want to's what they want me to lead it like. So that's sure okay by me.

I'm illegitimate and I'm a mulatto: I'm the child of a white mother that is, and I had a black father. I was raised by my mother's mother on a country farm in Kansas some place. I know nothing about my father, not one thing: not where he came from or where he went. My guess is I'm the result of what's called a one-night stand, and I should think it's possible he doesn't even know I exist. Soon after I was born my mother married someone else, and she gave me to her mother to look after me. I don't know anything about her either, since I've never heard from her or seen her from that day onwards so far as I know. Maybe when I was a baby she stopped by one time to look at me only she didn't like what she saw and decided not to bother with me no more and to leave me where I was. To me my grandmother's my mother and always has been, so I call her that: she's no husband and no children else, and when I was little I guess she put it around I was adopted or something. I don't give it too much thought; it's never caused me any problem, my genealogy hasn't, I mean.

What you might call my genetic history though, now that's a different matter. That's been a real big problem for me all through my life it has, specially when I was a kid. Because I'm not white, white people won't accept me as white, and because I'm not black, black people won't have me either as one of theirs. This has given me one hell of a hangup always. I mean not knowing which race I belong to, not knowing who you are racially; after a while you end up wondering whether you belong in the white race, the black race, or perhaps even if you belong to any part of the human race at all. At school white kids call you "Darkie" or "Blackie," and black kids shout "Whitey" at you: either way it hurts. A mulatto is a half-caste and a half-caste is an outcast, that was how it's always seemed to me. When I was with whites I wanted to be white, and when I was with blacks I wanted to be black, but I wasn't the one or the other. It was like I was visible at once to everyone that I wasn't one of them.

When you're young changes occur in your skin color too: you don't have no control of them, all you wish is they'd stop and make their minds up and settle down and stay permanently one way. There was a time around when I was ten or eleven and I started to go yellow: so much that other kids gave me the nickname "Tojo" a while. I didn't mind that if it was going to mean finally I was Hispanic, only it didn't, it went darker then lighter again and there I was still not knowing who or what in hell I really was.

With all those thoughts inside of me I guess as a result I never had no friends. Not in the way people are supposed to, to have other people you can confide in, discuss personal problems, things of that kind. Everyone dealt with me in the same way always, teachers as well as other pupils: they gave me a sort of amused tolerance all the time. I could see it on their faces, even before they started to speak. I was little too like I am now, I've always been this way. That's another thing gets you no respect; it makes people behave to you like you were a domestic pet. Their smile's a sort of friendly pat on the head. You resent it but you daren't show it that you do, because above all what you want's for them to like you and give you some respect. I wasn't a toy, I wasn't a pet, I was a bundle of fury most times I guess.

You saw it yourself at the show back there earlier: I sang them my song, I played them my tune, and they clapped their hands and smiled and I smiled back. They were saying to themselves Isn't he cute? Well no I'm not, and they wouldn't say that to themselves either, not if they knew what I was in here for. I'd like to have stood up and told them and say "So okay motherfuckers, you still think I'm cute? I raped an old woman. I fucked her and then I strangled her until she was dead. That's pretty cute isn't it? And you'd never think it would you, not of a little mulatto guy like me?"

Let me explain something for you so's there'll be no misunderstanding between us, okay? What we've been eating back there in the prison canteen before it closed up for the night was food. Food, human consumption fit for, right? The meat, if you were smart enough to find a piece of it in the hash, that could possibly have been mutton, and if it was, it was guaranteed to be fresh if that includes anything up to three years old. The potatoes were fully matured from the back end of last year's crop, the cabbage was genuine class B plastic, and the cinnamon doughnut was a good-conduct bonus for not throwing up the previous comestibles. You got it? Good, then we can go on.

At school I was a no-good: I was a no-good scholar, I was a no-good athlete or ball player, and I was a no-good person. That about sums it up. What I wasn't though was a bad person. I wasn't a bad person because to be a bad person when you're a kid you need friends, and those were what I didn't have. You need friends to lead you into bad ways, to let you join them and teach you bad things like taking dope and drinking alcohol and fornicating girls—all things like that which are normal and natural and greatly enjoyable. I didn't have no other kids though who'd let me join them, because I was a white Hispanic black like I've explained, so I had to be content with being happy as I was. That wasn't so difficult to do, because I kind of lived inside myself. I played a game of persuading myself everybody liked me because they were always smiling at me, even when I knew them smiling meant the opposite of what they thought.

Some days I attended school, and some days I didn't, I just went off with my friend and rode freight cars and hitchhiked on trucks and stuff like that. Him and me we understood one another and we got on fine. My friend was just like me, see—in fact he was me, so there was no problem there. There was one special place in particular we liked to go; it was an abandoned quarry three miles north of town. I don't remember what they'd ever been digging for there—ballast I think—only to us it was an old worked-out gold mine. We spent hour after hour scratching around in the dust and the dirt of it everywhere in case there was a nugget or two had somehow been missed, but there never was. And near it were some residences in a wooded area where retired millionaires lived. Least that's what we liked to pretend they were, people who'd made fortunes from the gold mine and then built themselves homes around the area, ready to jump back in and make more money from the workings if they ever came viable again. Some of the properties had hundreds of acres of land around them and security fences: the trappings of people who'd made it and were determined to hold on to it, you could say. Sometimes I go back there in my mind; not for any sentimental reason but not for bad-dream reasons either. It's a place I think about that's all, like it was in a movie I'd seen way back and remembered. That was the place I committed my crime.

Sure I'll tell you about it, why not? Twenty-one years ago which is when it was, that's a long long time. I may not have the details too clear anymore, but I'll remember those I can. I don't dwell on it, I don't talk about it, now I don't even give it much thought. I regret it for a lot of reasons though: it was the end of somebody's life and it was the end of mine. Only I don't say that with sadness or self-pity, only as a fact. What it's done is left me feeling bad about Thursdays, I guess that's its longest-lasting effect.

May two, May two twenty-one years ago: let's start like that. Central character one fifteen-year-old mulatto schoolboy, who's me. A sunny Thursday morning and he's at school, sitting in back of the class and looking out the window at the sky and chewing gum. What's in his head? I don't remember; nothing very much like always I shouldn't think. I expect he's wishing he was the fuck out of there and doing something more interesting, which is what he usually thought. But an idea's forming in his mind, that at break time that's where he'll be: not anywhere special, just the fuck out of there, which a half hour later is where he is, out the gate and down on the highway hitching a lift. Where to, anywhere, who cares? A truck pulls up and he climbs into the cab.

Cut to deserted workings in an old quarry, which looks like it might be part of an abandoned gold mine but it isn't. The boy's sitting on a rock someplace at the side in the shade, kicking his feet. He doesn't know what he wants to do next, except wait and find out what it is he wants to do. He looks around at nothing, and nothing looks back at him. Fade.

Funny, I can't tell it that way, it sounds unreal. It's a long time since I've given it any thought. That's what they all say isn't it: "It was unreal, it was like I was in a film, it was like I was outside of it watching myself"? Only no it wasn't like that, least not in my memory of it it wasn't. It wasn't real but it was real, so I guess I'm saying it was both. Anyway I reached a decision: I decided to trash a house, which was something I'd done a few times before. Not stealing from it or taking things, trashing it around a little that's all. My favorite thing was scratching wallpaper with something sharp, maybe a kitchen knife or a piece of glass I'd broke. Like this, criss criss on the paper so it hung down in long shreds. My second favorite thing was pissing on a rug, specially a nice white one. Only you could only do that at certain times, when conditions were right, when your bladder was full.

I'd not trashed any of those houses in that area before, because like I told you they had a lot of security or most of them did. A funny thing though was it was usually at the front: big gates, a high fence, cement walls. I think it was some kind of deterrent thing: you saw it all and you thought to yourself Wow, that looks well guarded, so you went away some place else. If you went around and looked in the back there'd be only a few strands of wire or overhanging trees, you could easily climb up and jump over. People with money are a bit crazy that way: they don't like spending on things people can't see, so they put everything up front and hope that'll frighten people off and maybe impress the neighbors some as well.

I did what I'd done before, walked around among some trees where no one could see me, stopped a while looking at a place or two to see if there was anyone home. It's a sixth sense you have, I don't know how it works, you get a feel if somewhere's occupied or not: something left on a patio that won't be there long, a drinks tray maybe or something like that, and you know someone'll be along soon to take it in. Or a book or a newspaper lying on a bench; people don't walk away and leave them, they're sure to be back. Finally I hit on a place which had all the right vibrations of somewhere empty, so I climbed the fence, went around the garage which didn't have no car in it, then took a chance on a ground floor sliding glass window not being locked, which it wasn't.

It was a good-quality place, nice furniture, lots of expensive stuff lying around. If I'd been a thief I'd have been excited by it. But I was a fifteen-year-old kid without ideas of financial advantage, a youngster wanted to leave his calling card that's all. Then I heard a sound. Someone was moving around somewhere upstairs and I realized I'd made a mistake. I ran out again back the way I'd come in, around the garage and over the fence and away. I was scared, scared as hell: I'd seen movies in which householders came at intruders with shotguns and I sure didn't want to be involved in anything like that. So like I said, I ran—a quarter of a mile or more maybe, and I didn't stop going till my breath gave out and I sat on a fallen tree in the woods.

But here's a strange thing now. Why does a natural coward suddenly change and decide he wants to be brave, can you tell me that? You know what I was when I was puffing and blowing and trying to catch my breath back sitting on that tree? I was ashamed of myself, that's what. Ashamed that the moment I heard a noise somewhere in the rest of the house I turned like I was chicken and ran. I didn't have even the dignity to walk at a rapid pace or anything, I just ran and ran. I'd done nothing to the house—there hadn't been time—and all

I'd thought of was getting out of there with all possible speed. That was a downright disgraceful thing for me to face: I'd been a coward, least that's what I looked like to myself. So I had to disprove it right there and then, I had to go back and find me another house and trash that one straight away. Nothing else would do, the coward had to prove himself to be brave. So I did, I went right back to find me some place else.

It didn't take long. I went to another house very similar only smaller than the first one; it was in the same direction too, which meant I had to walk back the way I'd come. Doing that kind of made me feel brave again: I'd show them, I'd show them I weren't no coward, that was the feeling I had in my head. Another one was anger: I got real mad at anyone thinking I was. Anger and bravery, bravery and anger: those are kind of funny feelings to have when all you're doing is trying to find some place to trash. No one's ever explained it to me where those feelings came from and how it was they took that form.

This time it was the kitchen I went in through, the back door wasn't locked and I just walked in. A door not locked: you'll say I should have known straight off there must be someone home. It was crazy of me not to think of that but all I was intent on was being brave and doing a little harm. The kitchen was big, very big and smart and modern I remember; it had a sort of a central cooking area and there were cupboards and worktops all around the walls. There was a kind of a barbecue grill under a copper hood, too, and everywhere shelves and polished wood doors. It was all nice and tidy. If you were looking for somewhere to start trashing, that would have been as good a place as any to begin.

But kitchens weren't my scene: they never have been, they were too much like home. Everyone has a kitchen, right, so where's the point of messing it? You want to leave your mark somewhere where there's more individuality about it and impress your own individuality on that. So I went on through and along the big wide hallway and turned at the end of it into a kind of a living area: there were chairs and sofas and long red velvet drapes at the windows and all stuff like that. It was someone's real comfortable home: I felt sad not having a place like that of my own.

Up over a brick fireplace at the side there were two sort of little antique swords and I pulled one of them down. It wasn't sharp so's it was dangerous, but it had a good point on it. I poked it around a bit, I knocked a pottery vase off a table and ripped some of the upholstery of the furniture and things like that. I really wanted to mess the place up good and I was looking forward to it. Then I saw a white long-haired rug on the floor by a piano, so I went over to it and unzipped my pants and started to piss on it: you know, very cool and deliberate and systematic. I wanted to ruin it.

I'd not heard nothing because maybe I'd been making too much noise myself, but then suddenly it hit me: someone had come in the room. I turned around and a woman was there, an old woman, she had white hair and a plain pink summer dress. She wasn't holding a weapon or anything but she didn't look afraid, she stood there and looked me straight in the eye. Then she spoke. Her voice I can't properly describe, but it came out like a sort of a venomous hiss. "What are you doing in my house nigger?" she said. She said it that special way white people have of talking to a person they think's black.

I took a step towards her but she didn't move, she didn't back off. I'm small but she was smaller; she was a tiny woman almost you could say. There was something about the fact she didn't look one bit frightened that made me suddenly feel mad. I took another step, and I saw her eyes move down to my pants and my dick hanging out from them: she looked at it and I felt it grow. I went at her in a rush and she fell on her back on a sofa and I jumped on top of her and raped her, and she hardly struggled at all. She just sort of gasped and screwed up her eyes while I went on and on doing it, then after a while she stopped gasping and started to moan and cry. When I'd finally finished I sort of rolled off her and slid onto the floor, I couldn't get my breath. She was lying there and sobbing with her hands over her face, and she was saying "Oh my God, oh my God, I wish I was dead, I wish I was dead." So I just said "Okay then" and I knelt up and put my hands round her throat and throttled her. It didn't take long: it seemed like only a minute and then she went limp like a kind of a stuffed doll. I think she made a little sort of a noise like a sigh that's all and that was it. "I wish I was dead": I guess she shouldn't have said that, it sounded like she was telling me what I should do.

I don't know how long I stayed in the house after that, I think it was quite a while. I've since thought about it sometimes; it was like I was waiting, like I expected someone to come along and take me away. One thing I did was walk down the hallway towards the kitchen. I saw a little shower room I'd not noticed before, so I took off all my clothes and had a shower and then got back dressed again and went. I didn't go back in the room where the woman was.

On the road I hitched another lift and went back into school. When I got there one of the teachers I knew was coming along the corridor towards the main door. She stopped me and asked me where I'd been because they'd listed me not being there that afternoon. I spoke to her just like we were having a normal conversation. I said "I've been up at the old quarry and I've killed an old woman in one of the houses, so I guess you'd best call the police." She said "Okay Vince, come on and sit in the office here and I'll fetch you some coffee" which I thought was pretty cool. She told me not to say anything to the police when they came unless someone else was with me there.

The police took me to the police station and put me in a room; they said for me to wait there on my own while they brought my mother. When she came three of them took me in another room with her and got out their notebooks: they told me to take my time and tell them every detail I could of what I'd done. But I shook my head, I said I wasn't going to tell them anything at all, not in front of my mother. I said I was only going to speak if she wasn't there and they brought an attorney for me. They argued with me about it a bit, but finally they agreed.

They brought a black guy who'd said he'd take the case. I told him and the police everything, including the fact the woman had called me a nigger; I figured that might get me a bit of sympathy from him. So far as I know it didn't though. I never heard mention of it again, not any time afterwards all the way through. It was fifteen months before I came to trial, and I pleaded guilty to both the charges, murder one and rape. Both carried the death sentence and for a while it looked like the only argument was going to be whether I should be executed or whether I shouldn't. I was fifteen when I did my crimes and there-fore too young for it, but sixteen by the time I was tried and by then I was old enough to be put to death. Finally it all became irrelevant: a new state governor was elected and he said he wasn't going to have no executions anymore. I don't recall I lost a lot of sleep wondering what would happen to me. I knew I'd be killed or incarcerated for ever, and whichever, it was not anything I'd have a say in. I suppose I'd sooner be alive than dead if someone was to press me on it, but I've not given it a lot of thought.

Neither have I given a lot of thought either to what you might call the circumstances of the crime and what caused it. A lot of other people have, they seem to be obsessed with it. Not me, I've lost count of how many psychiatrists have interviewed me, before the trial and time and time again after it for the first few years. But when they did, it always came down to the same question: "Why did you do it?" That was always the bottom line. My answer to it too was always the same: "I don't know why I did it, I thought you were supposed to tell me." I don't have any insight into it, and I don't have much remorse or regret for it either. I don't go over it in my mind, I don't relive it or anything like that. It was a set of facts, like I've told you, but it doesn't give me any pleasure either to think I was the one who performed them, or come to that it doesn't give me feelings of disgust or shame. It wasn't a very nice thing to do, sure, but the world's full of people who do things that aren't very nice, or have things done to them which aren't nice either, so what?

One guy ten years back, he was a psychiatrist who came to see me because he was doing a study of something or other: maybe it was of guys like me, I don't recall. I don't know what his name was and I don't know if he ever set down what he'd discovered or what he hadn't for people to read. And he said to me "You're a classic case you are, Vince" he said. "You fucked your mother and then you killed her." He didn't tell me what I was a classic case of, though. The woman looked nothing like my mother, and anyhow I love her so why should I want to kill her? My mother's my grandmother like I said, and she's my best friend and always has been. She writes me once a month and sends me newspapers and magazines, and she never fails or lets our contact fade. She's an old lady now of course, but I've never wanted sex with her or wished her any kind of harm. So where does all that fit in with what the shrink said to me? I can't make no sense of it, not in any way I can't.

You know what they're saying, all of these clever people, is the same: they're all saying that they can't find anything wrong with me. And you know I sure can't either, can you?

LISN BUD LISN

JEFF HESSLER

Excuse me sir, you looking for me? One three zero one seventy-nine Hessler, would you be looking for me by any chance? Yeah great, I'm glad to know you, how're you doing? Pull up a chair right here, gee I'm sorry about all this noise.

In a blue-and-white sweatshirt and faded jeans, he was sitting at a table in a small alcove at the side of the packed visiting room. A tall man with white scar marks on his face, he had cropped white hair and deep-set green eyes. He put his hand to his ear and lowered his head, trying to hear through the hubbub of people shouting and children screaming excitedly and running round between the benches and around the clattering metal chairs.

Pardon me? No sure I didn't mind having to wait for you sir, no not at all. The first visitor I've had come to see me in four years, it made a change to have something to wait for, honest it did, sure. Hell, I sure didn't imagine there'd be as many people around though as there are. Say, how'd it be if you moved your chair sideways next to me here?

A guard standing nearby stiffened and watched suspiciously, unfolding his arms and putting his hands on his hips before nodding permission for the move.

He's okay that guy, not like some. I've seen him before; he's always got to have me in his sight but he'll leave us alone. So how long are you reckoning to talk with me, a couple of hours? Sure we can do it in two parts, yeah sure that'll be just fine.

Sometimes at first when he was speaking he stopped suddenly, his attention distracted momentarily by the voice or the face or the movement of someone else in the room. He'd bring back his concentration with a quick shake of his shoulders, rubbing his chin and looking down at his fingers, repeating what he'd been saying and mumbling an apology. Later his voice quickened and his words tumbled out in a flood.

I'm not so good at talking with people these days. Sixteen years in one of these places doesn't do a lot for your self-confidence, mostly you don't say much more than you have to, and that's not a lot.

I'll begin again. I'm one three zero one seventy-nine Jeff Hessler, I'm forty-six and I've been incarcerated sixteen years. I came inside at the age of thirty with two terms of natural life, one for kidnap and one for murder, and both without parole. That means I'll never come out unless the state governor exercises clemency, and that's not something I can see happening this side of eternity, because I'm what's known as a very bad and violent and dangerous man. I am also, or maybe I should say I was also a different kind of very bad and violent and dangerous man, and for that I was a hero and got medals to prove it, so you can take your pick. Jesus this racket's really something isn't it, you'd think there was a war going on.

My background is I come from a very large family. As a matter of fact my mother was married three times and she had three children by each of her husbands and then she gave up—on husbands or having children, I don't know which. But I don't want to make it sound she was someone who didn't know her own mind or was promiscuous or anything of that sort. She wasn't, she was more the kind the Almighty if there is such a person kept dealing her a series of bum hands. Her first husband was in the military and got himself killed in Korea, her second husband was also in the military and ran off with a nurse he met when he was being treated in the hospital, and her third husband who was my dad, he was an air force base commander until he retired. He died just on twelve years next month. If that sounds like I come from a military background that'd be right because that's exactly true. Five of my brothers or half brothers have been or still are in the military, and ten or twelve uncles as well. That's our tradition and it's always been that way for three generations. Wherever there's a war you'll find the United States Army or Air Force or Navy, and wherever you find them you'll always find several Hesslers or their relations around.

When I was a kid I didn't like my dad too good, but my mother I always adored. She was kind and soft and gentle and very pretty too, and I think I was her favorite because I was her youngest one. I don't see her no more now and she doesn't write, but I think she still has a place for me in her heart. She used to come and see me a time or two but then she got sick with multiple sclerosis. I'm sure she'd have gone on coming if she could, but Alberta, Canada's where she lives now and that's a long way away. Two of my uncles write to me pretty regular though, and they used to send her money as well for her to come on a visit once a year. The last time I saw her though, well it was very painful for her, physically painful I mean. She said she'd come again when she was better, but I don't think she ever will be better, not now.

I think of her a lot, and I don't just have love for her like most kids have for their mas: I have something else, and that is respect. She was a fine character and a very remarkable one and I'll tell you why I say that: she bore five boys and four girls and she had plenty of suffering in her life, but through all of it she always treated every one of us equal, and made us feel we were all part of one big family, which was hers. She taught us filial bonding, all of us, and that can't have been no easy thing to do. There were times like Thanksgiving where somehow she brought us all together with one another under the same roof, and when she did, she always referred to one of the others as "your brother" or "your sister," there was this feeling that we all belonged. I've never had kids myself but I've often thought about if I did how hard it'd be not to have favorites and harder still not to show it. But if it was ever that way with her I was never aware of it, and I think if you spoke to any of the rest they'd all tell you the same. There's a character in a book *Anne of Green Gables,* I read it once but I don't know why because it's a kid's book, a girl's book, but it reminded me of her. Oh boy, what do you know, how about that: what'd the guys in my old outfit say if they knew I'd been reading a book for girls!

I guess my scholastic career wasn't especially a brilliant one, but that didn't greatly matter. As soon as I was old enough I went into military school because there was no question of me having anything else but a military career. Come to think of it it wasn't even discussed, not as far as I can remember. One of my brothers one time went into teaching, and another one was an engineer, but they were regarded as kind of oddballs who caused the rest of us puzzlement by not wanting to follow the family tradition. I sure did myself: I was proud of my background and patriotic, and I can remember all the time hoping that when I was old enough there'd still be a war somewhere for me to fight. But I needn't have worried, not knowing Uncle Sam. If we ever ran out of battles to fight we'd start one among ourselves. That Kissinger guy for example, they gave him the Nobel Peace Prize for getting us into some real damn good wars.

As soon as I was seventeen it was no more than two weeks at the most after graduating that I was at boot camp for my basic training. One of my uncles who had a high-up job as a recruitment department officer fixed it for me to go into the marines. That was a real great honor, it was what I'd set my sights on but never dared to dream of all along, and the family gave a party for me because it was such a matter for pride. My dad told me he was proud of it and meant it, he was never one for giving out false praise. My mother kissed me and told me she loved me and meant that too, and all my friends and relatives came from all over and shook me by the hand. I guess it's no wonder I thought myself someone special and pushed any thoughts of avuncular string pulling clean out of my mind.

I went for training as a boat coxswain, and I suppose though I say it myself I must have been a quick learner, because my very first posting was straight to a destroyer in the Pacific, and from there after only a few weeks to the allocation center at Pearl Harbor. I met guys there who were real cynics because of their own experience and who said that was as far as I'd ever get, but they were wrong in my case because when they asked for volunteers for active service in Vietnam I was about the first in line. It's not uncommon to come across guys like those ones. You know the sort: they say they've never been picked but don't tell you it was because they never actually put down their names. At the time I thought they were bullshitters and windbags and maybe even cowards at heart, but when you're only nineteen like I was then, you throw around judgments on people like they were grenades. It's when you get older you see they might have a point that you might call common sense, but at that age that was far too subtle for me.

I was given a couple of weeks' extra training in small-boat handling, and then I was on my way, posted on active service as an NCO to be in charge of an assault craft in a riverboat squadron. Things happened so quick it was difficult for me to take it all in. One week I was a callow youth and then the next one I was John Wayne, in charge of eight men and a million-dollar fighting boat. The anticipation, the excitement, the pride: you're so hyped up with it it's like you're high on drugs all the time. All you can think of is action action action, you've no thoughts of anything else in the world.

It's a dangerous state to be in, because somehow you have to let some of the steam out, else you'll explode. Sure they want your aggression and they'll get it, but first you've got to put it under control. So for the first week they keep your feet on solid earth and don't let you within a hundred miles of a fighting zone. They set you down in a camp on the edge of a river someplace and they tell you if you've got knowledge first of all they want you to spread some of it around. They give you a unit of eight men and they tell you these guys are going into combat with you in a few days, but to start off you've got to win their confidence because they've done no fighting yet and they're looking to you to demonstrate to them how to behave. It's true, the guys are inexperienced and scared too a bit, some of them, but what they've told them about you, that isn't true, not at all. They say you've seen plenty of combat yourself and they can rely on you to give them the benefit of what you know. That puts you on your mettle: these suckers are looking up to you, so you act in front of them what they want to believe. Your higher-ups are watching you too, to see how you handle yourself, to see if you can make it true what only them and you know is make-believe.

It's a basic idea and it's a good one, it makes you calmed down and cool. You're in charge of your men, you're in charge of yourself, and that's how it should be if you're going to win wars. Stay thinking, stay logical, stay aware. Give out hell when it's needed, and then immediately it isn't, turn off the tap. Well I learned it okay, and I learned it fast. By the week's end I wasn't nineteen, I was no age at all; I was that year's top-range model of a fighting machine.

I had two separate tours in Nam, of one year each with a couple of months that's all as a break in between. On the first one I saw action maybe two dozen times, and I'll tell you, my life was charmed: I got me a chest full of medals including a Purple Heart, a Bronze Star, a Vietnamese Medal of Valor and a whole host of other things for spreading death and destruction wherever I could. It was like it always is, the higher the body count you could claim the more decorated you were. I didn't enjoy it, I didn't not enjoy it, and I did it the best I was capable of because that was my job. I took risks and I saved lives, and if saving a life meant having to take others, well then that's what I did. I collected a couple of bullets, one in the shoulder and one in the leg, but they were flesh wounds and not serious, and both times in ten days I was back fighting again. What I'd say was I was an example to others, and that's something they liked and gave me those decorations for. An example of giving no thought to myself and putting others first, like by killing them while giving no thought to danger I was putting myself in, do you see what I mean?

When they sent me back on leave to Honolulu at the end of that first year's tour, I didn't want to go: I was obsessed with what I was doing, it was all I was living for. I'd heard rumors too: that when you got there they held out blandishments to you to take stateside duty for a while. I didn't know what was going on then, but I think I do now: they wanted some returning live heroes to help with the enlistment drives. Even if I'd known that then though I wouldn't have bought it. There was still only the one place I wanted to be, and that was where there was war. That was the real world and I wanted to get back to it. I was entitled to six weeks' furlough but I couldn't hack it, I stopped in Hawaii only two.

Oh, you know what, this noise here's so heavy I have to take a break from it, it's splitting my skull. It's more than a year I've been where there were so many people around. You can come back tomorrow in the morning can you? Well then I'd sure appreciate that, I really would. First thing'll be fine, there'll be no other visitors, we can just sit quietly in here on our own. I'll try and remember to bring you something I'd like you to see: it's a poem by that guy they always spell his name with small letters, e. e. cummings he's called, you know his things? See you tomorrow then, friend—eight o'clock. Sure okay then, nine.

ygUDuh

    ydoan
    yunnuhstan

    ydoan o
    yunnuhstan dem
    yguduh ged

    yunnuhstan dem doidee
    yguduh ged riduh
    ydoan o nudn
LISN bud LISN

dem

gud

am

lidl yelluh bas

tuds weer goin

duhSIVILEYEzum

You get it? Neither did I till someone explained it for me, no. What it is is his imitation of an American soldier, sitting drunk some place like in a bar. You need to read it out loud, very slow and slurred like the fat pisshead's saying it to anyone who'll listen to him, see? The mighty American soldier telling the world what we're going to do to those liddle yelluw bastuds—we're gonna civilize them!

Pretty neat huh, yeah I'll say. I read somewhere someone once said Cummings was the most cynical writer about the United States there ever was, and I'd go along with that. He was referring to the Korean not the Vietnam War, but it'd have been even more true of those like me who were fighting that if he had. Those people we fought and killed so many of and in their own country, they were people we were doing it to to benefit them, that's what we honestly thought.

LISN bud LISN, it haunts me it does. I get crazy still like it was yesterday when I think about my second tour. I couldn't wait to get back to it and I was more homicidal even then than I'd been on the first. I'll tell you what I had: deep and all the way through me, it was blood lust, that's what it was. I wanted to kill. My only enjoyment in living was causing other people's death. And I'll tell you something straight too: they weren't by any means all of them or not even most of them fighting men like we were, bristling with weapons. The majority were civilian peasants in villages, women and children and sick old men. They weren't doing no harm to no one; they had no weapons and they couldn't defend themselves, and whenever and wherever we came across them, we didn't ask questions or offer mercy, we slaughtered them every single one. I can't estimate for you how many there were. What I will say is that some days and nights we answered calls for assistance from people on our own side, but if there weren't any of those other nights we went out searching for people from the other side and for the fun of it killed them instead.

It went on not quite another year, and then I was wounded in combat. I was taking my boat on a dawn raid on a village we'd located which we hadn't known about before. We decided on a quick hit on it and then away. It was on a beach at a jungle riverbank, and how it came about that some Cong were there I don't know. All we were thinking of was just doing a harmless routine exercise of killing us some unarmed civilians, that's all. Six yards or a little more maybe before the shore we took two mortars one after the other plumb amidships, then seconds after that we were raked from stem to stern with machine-gun fire. It wasn't cowardice made me back off, it was training and experience, but as I tried to make the turn another mortar shell hit on the waterline right by my side. I took fragments in my back and my arm and my head, which caused in the end partial loss of vision in this eye and some damage to my hearing. All told they said I needed four hundred stitches in different parts of me. I guess if I'd not been fortunate I'd have bled to death. Or maybe it was unfortunate instead that I didn't—that could be said. Out of it all came somewhere for me a second medal for bravery, which has to show something I guess.

I was taken to the hospital in Pearl Harbor where they did plastic surgery of various kinds. Altogether I was a year on my back, and after that there was no choice or chance for me, I was given a medical discharge and scheduled for home. I hung around a few months on recuperative medical leave and then flown back to San Francisco to be greeted with the biggest shock I've ever had. The anti-Nam protest movement was something I hadn't even heard of, but a section of it numbering hundreds of people was out there waiting for service men's return on every plane that flew in. People were shouting and waving banners, and when we crossed into the main building to go to our transport for base camp another great jeering mass had somehow got into there. The police couldn't handle it and neither could the military, and we had to walk through a gauntlet of milling people surrounding us on every side. They were screaming and actually spitting at us, some of them: it was like you were in a house of horror, you couldn't believe it, no one had prepared you for it, not in any way. You'd come home proud, thinking yourself a hero and that you'd be welcomed with glory and praise, and here you all were, you and your comrades some of them walking on crutches or lying on trolleys, being greeted like you were some kind of terrible monster, some kind of scum.

If that shook you up, what followed in the weeks afterwards was worse. Instead of parties and celebrations and people slapping you on the back and wanting to shake your hand, you were treated everywhere like you'd contracted some terrible infectious disease. While I was waiting for my final discharge papers to come through to the camp I never wore my uniform when I went out down into town. I still had plenty of visible scars on my neck and my face and I walked with a limp; when I went in a cafe or a bar, if anyone asked what'd happened to me I'd tell them it was a road accident. But I guess that was such the standard stock explanation that people had heard they'd look at you and say you'd been in Vietnam hadn't you, and when you said yes that was the end of the conversation.

What friends I'd had in my life until then, they'd all of them been in the military, and they were the only ones I knew how to talk to, so soon I started staying in camp all the while. I'd no relatives or family anywhere near, and I felt like I was completely on my own. Then a guy on the base told me of a place he went in town where he said I'd find friends, so evenings I started going there. It was a gambling and strip joint with drugs and girls, and I had myself one hell of a good time. You know how I mean? Keep telling yourself when you're there "Boy oh boy, I'm having one hell of a good time, I'm having one hell of a good time!" You don't end up persuading yourself of it, but you keep on trying all the same.

There was a girl I met there one night and she took to me, and I did to her. It was all the conventional stuff because I was a soldier and the only way I could think was exactly the conventional way. She had two young kids and her husband had left her, and all she wanted out of life was not to be a stripper anymore but just stay home. All I wanted was not to be a soldier anymore but just to have a nice family to settle into, and here it was, one already made. So I moved in with her for a while, and it was a disaster right from the start.

Her kids were two boys, one of them ten and the other one eight, and she'd built me up to them like I was a hero returning from the wars. They were all the time asking me to tell them stories about my fighting adventures and that was the side of my life I wanted to forget. I found myself getting more and more bitter and angry with them about it.

They didn't understand. They brought home kids from school to meet their new dad and show him off, and some days I'd end up shouting at them and telling them the war hadn't been anything Americans should be proud of, it was a crime against humanity and they ought to be ashamed. Half the time I didn't understand why I felt like I did about it and the other half I felt bitter that good friends I'd had in Nam had given up their lives for their country and now we were despised and condemned. I was, I was totally fucked up in my mind.

I took to not going home, staying out all night and getting myself stoned on drugs and sleeping around. The girl I was supposed to be living with permanently, Janice, she told me either to stay with her or find myself someone else, but she wasn't prepared to share me like that. So I was only with her three months and then I took off and left her for good. What was at the root of it wasn't either drugs though or other women, it was money: I didn't have any and I needed to find work.

That's not so easy for a half-fit drug addict who's a Vietnam vet who nobody wants to know. When two guys up the West Coast in Seattle offered to take me in their business with them, I was glad of the chance. My family was living in Calgary, and I figured being closer to them so's I could pay them a visit once in a while would be good for me, kind of bring me back closer to my childhood and give me more of a chance to settle down. It didn't work out that way but that was my fault not theirs: I went to stay with my ma a couple of times but there was a restlessness in me that I couldn't explain. I guess it was six months at least I didn't see her at the end.

The work I was in was strictly illegal. I'll not say too much detail about it because others were involved, and only the half of it anyway came out in my trial. It was running drugs by boat, mostly up the coast to Vancouver, but sometimes the other way down the coast, a time or two as far south as Mexico. It was a big operation and a well-organized one. We had a deep-sea vacation travel company we built up as cover, and some of our boats were as big and well equipped as those I'd handled in Nam. I was two years doing that and I enjoyed the life: big money, adventure, skill, night landings, everything except being under fire, and I could do without that part of it or at least I thought I could. I had a girl or two in different places as well, but without strings attached, so my health and my life generally showed improvement all round.

But like they say, all good things come to an end, and for me it was sudden and final, and not something I'm proud of to tell. If you live the kind of life like I was doing you're always vulnerable to the human factor, and that was what brought me down. One of the guys in the organization I worked for had a girl: she was blond with long legs and I've always been susceptible to pretty faces on top of good figures, and I fell. She did a little too, I think; at least there wasn't much resistance from her whenever he was away. She had a big apartment on the beach in a fashionable place by the ocean, two cars and a pool, but I guess she felt her life wasn't complete any time she didn't have a man. She was a nice girl, an independent sort. It'll sound strange I guess for me to say it but I did, I liked her quite a lot. If she'd been the marrying kind, and I had, who knows how things'd have turned out.

But well, accidents happen, they happen all the time, and some of them can be very unfortunate in the consequences they have. Life was good like I said, and then I got bad news—really bad news it was, the worst. It was that the law was on my tail. And it wasn't no rumor either, it was grade one information which I got from an unimpeachable source, right from the very top of the tree. From the law itself is what I mean. I was told, and I double-checked it with another high-up in the vice department, and he told me the same thing, so I had to know it was true. Some folks would be surprised to hear something like that, but they shouldn't be: there's big big money in 'drugs and it's split all ways, and the law likes its share.

So who was giving them the information, that was the question, and the finger pointed only one way, and that was at my pretty lady friend. The only thing I've never been able to figure out though is why: not in all these years I've had to think about it have I felt I knew that. Maybe she was a plant, maybe the police had something on her themselves, maybe she was a highly placed operative for the law and had worked for them all her life. Maybe, maybe, maybe, is all I can say. A dangerous life for a lady to live: she must have known that herself, she surely must.

When I knew who it was for certain, I had to stop it for sure. That's one of the rules. You take the risk, you pay the price. Some things are unthinkable, but they have to be thought. If she'd been my mother, well it'd have been just the same. She had to be dealt with and it had to be by me because I was the one who knew. I couldn't discuss it with anyone first either, because that'd be telling a third person and that was another source of danger for you then you see, so it couldn't be allowed.

I went at night to the lady's apartment, I let myself in because I had my own key, I got her out of bed where she was asleep, and I took her away in my car. A long way away nearly all through the night, I won't say where. We sat and watched the morning sun come up over the desert, we kissed good-bye, I made her get out of the car and walk a few steps away, then I got out of it myself and followed her, and I shot her dead.

It took nearly a whole week for them to find me and come and

nail me. And you know what did for me finally? It's crazy: the special
kind of sand there was at that desert, they found some grains of it on
the soles of my shoes. There was no arguing about it, and that was it.
Two life terms like I said, one for kidnap and one for murder: and
here I am and here I'll stay, and that's the end of the story.

The poem, that one there by Cummings, I take it out and read it
to myself sometimes and it makes me think: I guess it's the incoher-
ence of it sums me up but I can't explain. I was a soldier, a man of
action: and thinking, well that's like I read somewhere, thinking's the
hell of the action man just like action's the hell of the man of thought.

There's only one way I see it, I've had a long time to think about it
that's for sure, and the way I see it it looks like this. They invested a lot
of money in training me, right? And they trained me good to get me
like they wanted, which wasn't a human being but a well-tuned killing
machine. Kill. Don't ask questions, don't think about it afterwards:
kill. I did it so well they gave me medals for it, and I went on day after
day doing it almost to my last drop of blood. And when I stopped they
used up more dollars still and mended me and made me back into a
human again and made me whole. But they paid no attention to what
was inside that body, which was a different kind of a hole. It was one
where there used to be a human mind. It had taken them years to
train that mind so that it'd respond to danger in one way alone, to
make it give an answer in the face of danger which was to have no
other thought but kill. Does this make any kind of sense?

I never for one moment considered any alternative for that lady
did I, it was the only way I was trained to react? I removed her,
instantly without giving the matter any other kind of thought. What
they'd put into me was cancer of the brain, and when they finished me
they never bothered to take it out again and replace it with any good
thing, they left it as a hole. I'm not saying I'm not to blame. I am and
will be, like others they taught to think the same way, but it was them
in the first place, they were the ones who put it into me, the violence
of our lives. LISN bud LISN . . . you hear what I'm saying? Yeah.

A FIGURE IN
THE SHADOWS

JOHN JOSEPH JAMES

*The venetian blinds at the windows of the small modern confer-
ence room of the administration block were half closed to keep
out the brightness of the afternoon sun. It was difficult at first to
distinguish much of him where he sat at the end of the polished table
with a small bowl of fresh fruit in front of him and a jug of iced water
with two polystyrene beakers on a tray. A trim elderly black man with
white hair and an eye patch, he wore gray slacks and a neatly pressed
blue shirt with a button-down collar and maroon-colored tie. Precisely he
realigned a manila folder after he'd extracted a typed sheet from it and
put the paper on top. His voice was courteous and quiet.*

This is something I wrote down last night when they told me you
were coming, and one of the young ladies in the administration office
where I work kindly typed it out for me today. I'll read it to you. I
wasn't sure when it came to talking if I'd find the right words, and it's
the most important thing I want to say. It's what I'd describe as my
prison philosophy which I'd like you to understand.

For the person who lives in permanent incarceration, incarceration is no punishment at all. Punishment is no longer punishment, it becomes something else entirely and exists quite
separately and on its own. By itself it has no meaning because it
no longer applies to the person it's applied to unless he himself
chooses that it should. It satisfies society perhaps, but does noth-

ing to the prisoner: it's lost all meaning for him, and therefore in
that particular context he's free.

It still doesn't quite say what I'd like it to but it comes as near as I
can get. I'll put it back in the folder for you, take it with you when you
go. It has a list of dates in my life story and some cuttings about my
crimes. Keep it if it's of interest: it'll tell you all there's to say about
John Joseph James. It's basic in one very simple thing: he's a man
who's to spend his whole life in prison and will stay there till it ends.

I don't know how many others you've spoken with or what
they've said, but I'd guess with most of them that they've mentioned
hope somewhere along the line. Would I be right, they're hanging on
to it somehow, because it keeps them alive? Let me say to you at the
start then that I don't have that. Please accept it and take it how it's
meant. It's not a cry to you either, nor one of despair. I've taught
myself to live without it and it's truly irrelevant. It's like I've tried to
express on this piece of paper here, and it means I now feel free.

I accept that I'll die in prison. There's no alternative for the system
except to have me do that, and there's no alternative for me either but
to accept: and that's a fact. It maybe sounds strange to say I agree with
it being so, but I really truly do. Once twenty-one years back it might
have been different, but not anymore. I'm not saying it would have
happened but there was a faint chance of them considering an application if I made one for a hearing for parole. Only right then, at that
moment I killed again: so no application could go forward, it would
have been absurd. I got another life instead, and that meant the end.
In my record here I'm giving you it shows I've killed two people: I've
been given two life sentences one after the other, plus thirty years
consecutive on a charge of attempted homicide. The odd thing about
it though is I'm not a dangerous man. If I was they wouldn't let me be
on my own here with you. That's because Assistant Warden Martin
who fixed it, he knows me pretty well and knows I'm no danger, he
knows I've settled down.

One time I thought I might write my life story myself, or some of it, but I don't think so now. If you're interested I'll tell it you, and you use it how you will. If you like an apple or a banana or something, please help yourself, it's all good and fresh. I'll look back through these papers a minute so I can keep it in order. Okay right then, let's see how it goes.

My name's John Joseph James and I'm just gone sixty-five. I've been incarcerated now continuously for thirty-five years. My first sentence was natural life for killing a policeman; nineteen years after I murdered another prison inmate so I had life for that as well. At the same time they charged me with the attempted homicide of a prison guard and gave me thirty years to follow. It all adds up to I don't know what, except I'll be here forever plus a day.

I'm an ordinary man, and I was an ordinary child. Like a million other black kids, I grew up in poverty, in an old tenement brownstone which we shared with four other families in a run-down part of a city on the coast of Alabama. My mother was a drunk. She had five children all by different men, and the one she had me with lived in another part of the house and had kids by different women too. I was never exactly sure who he was though, my father, because the situation was always confused. Different people were coming and going all through my life: sometimes they were there only a week or a month, and sometimes less than that.

I don't think when you're young you ever understand properly about adults and how they lead their lives, and after a while I guess you stop trying to. They have their world which is theirs and you don't ask questions about it and they don't encourage you to. My main special friend was a boy of my own age called Melvin who lived in the same house. Sometimes he and me talked about grown-ups together and their peculiar ways. I don't think we came to any conclusions except possibly one: it was that he and I might be related to each other, maybe we were half brothers even, or something like that. That was because one of the men who lived in the house seemed like he was especially nice to us whenever we met. He'd put his arms round both our shoulders and sometimes give us money for ice creams and tell us we were fine good boys. There were times when he and my mother behaved as though they were sweet on each other, I'd see them kissing and cuddling together on the stoop. But there was another woman in the house too he behaved with the same way exactly, and she was Melvin's ma. I think she might have been my mother's sister, but neither seemed to mind him being affectionate with the other one.

The situation never caused me and Melvin worry, that I clearly recall. So long as we had food and somewhere to call our home, the details of which of us belonged where and whose child he was didn't seem important at the time. And for that matter it wasn't different from the backgrounds of most other kids we knew. Melvin and me we had other things to think about, they were our concerns: playing in the street or just generally running around. Mine wasn't an unhappy childhood, feeling neglected or sorry for myself is something I don't ever recall. Life was always sunshine. As a kid adults left you alone to enjoy it and that was fine because always it was like there weren't any regulations or silly things like laws.

For the whole first ten years of my life one thing I've no memory of was school. I guess there must have been some for me but it's not a thing I have any memory of in any way at all. My recollection may be faulty here, but I don't think it is. Me and Melvin were in a permanent state of unrestriction or supervision you could say. We weren't delin-quents: we'd go into dime stores and maybe take a few cookies or candies, but never anything more. Hot days we'd go to a creek we knew of and fish or swim and throw stones, and our biggest adventure was to hitch a truck ride down to the ocean. There was a part that was north of the town and clear of the poor dirty quarter where our house was, and we'd go out there whenever we could and run around on the beach.

It was a strange sort of relationship because one thing we didn't do much of ever was talk: we had an understanding of each other that didn't need words. I knew most times what Melvin was thinking with-out having to ask him, and he was the same with me. Mornings when we met up we didn't discuss where we'd go or what we'd do: without saying anything we'd head for the same place, the creek or the beach or wherever, or go climb our rock. That was a special place we had there—we'd scramble way up to the top of it where there was a deep narrow defile in it facing out to sea. No one could see us on it and we'd sit hours under a ledge that overhung part of it and gave us some shade. We'd look out over the ocean and sit watching the waves where they broke at the foot of the rock below us in a great mass of foam. Some days we'd be there and neither of us would say a word, or sometimes we'd talk in a disconnected way about anything that came into our minds. And then something happened, I'm afraid.

I guess I don't know how to say the next part, or even if I should. There's nothing about it in the notes here, and I spent a long time last night thinking about if I would. It was a long time ago, but if you're to have the full picture you ought to hear it all I suppose. The time I'm talking about is fifty years past so its details aren't too clear.

He looked down at the closed folder and thoughtfully ran his finger- tip across it, slowly tracing a row of invisible lines. There was a long silence. He poured and sipped some water, turning the beaker reflectively in his hand.

We'd gone out to the ocean like we often did—June I think it was or maybe July. And this day was very unusual because for some reason I've never understood Melvin wanted to talk. He didn't so much want to have a conversation with me as tell me something he had on his mind. The subject was a girl and her name was Barbara Anne. She lived somewhere in the same house we did, but where I don't properly recall. He talked about her and he said he was in love. It seemed to me ridiculous then, and it still does now. I believe she was older than he was and by a good few years, and I thought him a fool. I guess what specially made me angry with him though was he started to tell me sex things he and she had done. I didn't think you should talk like that and tell your secrets to other people: and I remember feeling as well it was disgusting, and I didn't want to hear. I'd no time for girls myself and I hadn't thought Melvin had either. The best way I can describe my feelings about it was I felt I'd been betrayed.

Speaking about it now such a long time after it's as though I'm describing someone else who wasn't me at all. Whether I was jealous or confused about it is difficult to say. I can't re-create what was in my mind but I know it was all in a whirl. Before long I couldn't properly hear his words and I wanted him to stop. It seemed like he was saying too he was closer to someone else now, and what had been between us was coming to an end. He wasn't looking at me while he was talking, he was sitting like he always did with his eyes on the water and the waves.

So he never knew what happened, or so I've always thought: it was that I put my leg out towards him with my foot here in his back, and gave him a push. That he was so near the edge of the part of the rock we were on was something I never even thought about: but he sort of went forward like this and landed on his head a hundred feet below. He hit on a big boulder that was at the water's edge: then he lay there a moment, then slid off into the water and completely disappeared. I've relived it in my mind I don't know how many times: but the one conclusion I've reached about it has always been the same. I hadn't meant to kill him so it was an accident is what I'll always say. What I'd done was reacted to his words—quickly and without consideration of a consequence, of that much I'm sure.

But what followed afterwards, that was quite a different thing. Because it was that nothing happened, nothing of any kind. I didn't climb down to the bottom of the rock where he'd fallen to see if he was there. I didn't go down the other side of it either to the beach and tell someone and ask for their help. All I did was stay sitting like I was frozen, staring at the waves. It was like I'd watched something happen of which other people had been part that was separate from me and in no way my concern. I found that very strange.

When I did go home at the end of the day without Melvin with me, I don't recall now what I thought. Nobody asked me about him either, so I didn't have to give anyone an explanation about it at all. Maybe if they had I would have come up with something true or something false, there's no way of knowing: what I recall is that all the people in the house were taken up with something else instead. It was the man I'd thought my father and possibly Melvin's too had been taken off to jail; the police had come that day and arrested him and another man for dealing in drugs. It meant no one noticed Melvin wasn't there and that he'd disappeared.

That's how it was in the black quarters of a lot of cities in those days—there was no one to keep tabs. Family groups were splitting up and re-forming, then splitting again, it went on nearly all the time. The authorities only paid attention if there was trouble and there were kids on the loose. I remember a black social worker came to me soon after and told me they were making inquiries to try and find me a new home because my mother had been hospitalized. And it was from that point onwards that my life completely changed.

I was put into the care of a family in a different part of the state: in every way it's possible my life was turned around. I think the wife was some distant acquaintance of my mother's I believe, and she and her husband treated me in a way from then on no one had ever done before. They had no children of their own and both of them had a professional background. They were white and churchgoing, she was a teacher while he was a photographic studio supervisor with a mail-order catalog concern. They were very kindly people with a big house and two cars, and some years afterwards I learned they'd had a son the same age as me who'd had leukemia and died. In that sense I was a substitute but I never felt I was; they made me feel I was someone special to them but in my own right.

I don't know what basis she had for saying it, but more than once the wife would tell me she knew I had potential to achieve great things. I don't mean she had fancy ideas in any way, but she lost no opportunity to give me confidence. For a kid like I was, from the background I came from, she gave me a new way of looking at life that up till then I'd never knew there was. Their house was full of books and pictures and it was a whole new world, as different from the one I came from as living on the moon. It changed my life and when I think back about it now, it's almost like it was a dream. The biggest thing of all in it was it gave me self-respect: somehow those two people put it into me that I wanted to learn and be an educated person and someone who could hold his head up in the world.

The cut-off point in my mind was all that had gone before: the squalor and pointlessness of the life that I'd lived in, I wiped it all out. You write words in pencil on a piece of paper and then take an eraser to them and start over, it was something like that. In time I never thought any more about where I'd come from or who I'd been: I was a new kind of person entirely, you know what I mean? One thing I put out of my mind and never gave a thought to for years was the accident with Melvin. I couldn't see I should have reminded myself of it because what was the point, who even cared? I didn't myself: and sometimes I thought I'd imagined it and it'd never occurred.

My foster parents put me through high school, and college after that. In this great American society of ours everyone'll tell you anything is possible for everyone, it's the land of opportunity and everyone starts the same. That's correct, but there's something to add: you can have everything you want and reach whatever height you like, only so long as you've got the money, that's the part that counts. All through my schooling I knew exactly my aim, but if I hadn't had those wealthy people behind me I'd have had to lower my sights. From sixteen onwards my aim was the law. It was an attainable ambition but only because of the background I had. The poor kid I was in the earlier part of my life would never have had such a thought.

I don't know why law appealed to me, because of the precision and logic of it, that's it, I suppose. There was something about it I just felt was right: order out of chaos, let's put it that way. Something about the certainty of it, being able to apply rules and not make choices of your own: diligence, application, such things as that. I was a very orderly person in my teenage years, clean and well dressed. I didn't like parties, I didn't make friends, I was impersonal and I lived by the book. There was a part of me I kept hidden, and let nobody near. I didn't like emotion, that was something else too. It wasn't so much I had control of my feelings as I didn't have them the way other people did. I don't think that was a bad thing, I'd almost say it was good. When a tragedy did happen to me if I hadn't been like I was I could have gone right off the rails.

What I'm referring to now was something which came at me totally unexpectedly out of a clear blue sky. I was at law school in my final year and one night I had a message to say my foster parents had been in a motor accident and both of them killed. To someone else they'd have taken it I guess in a number of ways: but to me it was an announcement of fact. I had no control over it and so I turned my back. I was in the middle of final examinations and I had a job lined up to start: so the way it looked to me was all I could do was continue with my life. Sure I felt sad and grateful and all the other things: but in the year before it happened I'd been conscious and so had they that our lives were going separate ways.

There were things to arrange and things to be done, with the house and their affairs. But not much that couldn't be handled by the bank they'd appointed as their executors, and in six months it was all wrapped up and I was completely on my own. I benefited a little financially but no serious money was involved. Their insurance paid my final debts and fees and the bulk of their estate they'd left to their church.

The position I'd been offered was with a firm of corporate lawyers who had offices on the east coast of Florida and one of my professors was connected with them. So from school I went on to there. I was with them two years and all I did was work. Then they expanded into West Virginia and offered me a senior post. To have the opportunity they offered and still be comparatively young, in a lot of ways that seemed to me like I was living out a dream. In ten years I'd been given chances and taken them, and I'd come up from a slum to a position where the future had so many options and opportunities I couldn't believe.

I've said it before and I'll say it again: you can never imagine though how things can turn around, and in my case they did and made no kind of sense. Those ten years of achievement vanished in ten seconds or less. Something occurred which I don't see as having anything to do with me yet all my future disappeared: it's hard to understand. It was like someone blew out a candle and left me in the dark.

Every morning I drove to work from my apartment along by the beach, then turned off it onto the highway near to where my office was. It was a half-an-hour drive and I was so familiar with it I'd do it most days without ever thinking or watching my speed. If the traffic was stationary at an intersection I was never impatient, I'd sit there and wait: if the lanes were clear I'd roll along like the rest. This morning I'm talking of I was exceeding the limit a little and when I looked in my mirror I saw a motorbike cop right there on my tail: then he pulled out around me and waved me down. I stopped, and he stopped, just a little ahead. I guess if he'd given me a ticket that would have been all that happened: but what he decided was that all he would do is warn me instead. I don't remember his face because he'd a helmet on, and I don't remember his words: but I felt suddenly angry with him and not wanting to hear what he said. I was wanting him to stop the same way all those years before I'd wanted Melvin to as well.

He turned his back on me I remember, that much was clear in my mind, and I can see him now, the way he walked back to his motorcycle and got on it again. My car engine was running and I put my foot down on the gas. I don't think he ever knew what hit him and I just mowed him down. I did it to him too like I'm telling it now, without any emotion or violence or any regret: in pure cold-bloodedness was what they said at my trial. I'd say they were right: after I'd hit him I didn't stop to see what I'd done, I pulled out into the traffic again like nothing had happened, and gave it no thought. In another twenty minutes like I did every day I was sitting at my desk. I was dictating answers to letters when the police arrived and put me under arrest.

Sometimes I've wondered what line I'd have taken if I'd been a defending attorney and assigned to my case. Would I have gone for some kind of insanity plea on the grounds it was such an irrational and inexplicable act? Well no, I think not. For months after it happened while I was waiting for trial I never tried to explain. The price I'd paid for being stopped for a minor traffic violation was the thing no one could understand, and least of all me. I pleaded guilty, I got life without parole. If at that time they'd had executions I'd have been put to death I'm sure. There are killings and killings, and as far as the law's concerned killing a policeman is one they'll never hear any excuse for, as everyone knows.

I have to go now for an hour, I have an appointment with an ophthalmic nurse who comes in at a quarter after four. If you'd like us to go on talking a while after that then I gladly would, sure. Have some fruit and read my notes.

When he came back again he took another chair from those at the table and sat astride it near a window, pulling a string to open a blind and allow in more light.

I've glaucoma, the sight's more or less gone now for good out of this eye. The nurse from the hospital here's a sweet young kid, we have laughs together often me and her. I tell her so long as I can still see her I don't greatly mind. You know what she said to me one time? "Remember the old proverb now, J.J.," she said. "In the country of the blind men, the one-eyed man is king."

Thirty-five years of continuous imprisonment, what's new to be said on that? Monotony, indifference, I guess those'd be my words. Prison's its own society, it has its own life and it has its own rules. When I first came in on my life term, like I'd done on the outside I had some ambitions for myself and wanted respect. But inside's the place you have to rethink about things like that: you have to forget them and give up wanting things you can't attain and learn to not want them anymore. I think I was the best educated man in the place when they first incarcerated me, or thought I was, so it didn't take me long to recognize that anyone sentenced for killing a police officer was way down the bottom of the list when it came to parole.

So I didn't hope. I accepted the reality I was inside for good. If I had any thoughts of doing something with my life, then they'd got to focus on inside. It wasn't hard: the only things I thought of were prison things, and the only people I thought of were prisoners. If someone came to me saying he didn't know how he was going to do his time, I helped him all I could. I listened to what he had to say and I tried to get him to think realistically about himself and his position and his time. I was the first man to start a Lifers' Association and I became its president, and what I was doing was good and worthwhile: the most important part of it was it wasn't an organization that dealt in false ideas. I think people respected that, I really think they did. I built it up and carried it on for something more than twenty years.

The only ones I could never help though let me tell you, they were the innocent ones. I don't know how some guy who's serving a sentence for something he didn't do can take it: to wake up in the middle of the night and know you're in prison and will stay there, that must be a special kind of hell, one to end them all. I know what I've done and how I got to where I am: I've said always I've deserved it and I believe that and it brings a kind of peace. If I didn't know that then it would rot me to my soul.

The other matter, the one I spoke of earlier, when another inmate died, it would look to anyone outside I suppose I must be very violent, what other word can be used? It wasn't in this prison and it was a time when like I told you, if it hadn't happened there's a chance but not much more that I'd be given leave to apply for parole. It's hard for me to remember the details of the circumstance and I don't want it to sound like I'm making excuses because I'm not. But one thing about prison is you have to obey its rules. I don't mean the official ones of the authority that's running it but those of the inmates themselves. There was this guy who didn't, and feelings were high. It was difficult, difficult for me I mean, because he was my friend. In fact I'd say personally he got as close to me as anyone had ever got. We're not talking about the so-called real world outside don't forget: you can have friendships and closeness with people here inside that are just as real.

Without going into the detail of it he wanted to escape, and he'd worked out a plan. I didn't want him to go and I'll say no more than that. I thought it was crazy because it involved some other guys I knew weren't reliable and all he'd get was hurt. If you look in these papers of my record there what it'll tell you is I quarreled with another inmate and I killed him with a knife. It won't tell you what for or how it came about: a statement of the fact but not why it occurred. This is prison and no one wants to know anything like that: lock people up and keep them inside. What crimes there are in prison, there's no great concern.

The young man I'm telling you of, there's little else to say. He was killed by me in broad daylight without any attempt at concealment and a guard was involved. He tried to intervene and I knocked him to the ground. I threatened him and they made that up to the other charge, of attempted homicide. Some other guards jumped in and I took blows to my head, but they were charged with nothing because that's how it is. I don't have bitterness about any of it now though, and I don't have regret. I live out the rest of my time in prison here, and inside my head.

He stood up and walked to the door in response to a knock, then unhurriedly turned back for a moment with a smile and a nod. His handshake was firm. "Good to meet you," he said.

PEOPLE LIKE ME

HANK SULLIVAN

*T*he security checks at the entrance to the inner cell block were comprehensive, stringent and intense.

Letters of authority and permissions to enter were examined line by line and compared with copies already held on file. Passport and driving license were closely scrutinized, numbers authenticated, photographed and then retained. Signatures were matched, distinguishing physical characteristics such as eye color and complexion were studied and noted. All jacket and trouser pockets were emptied and left hanging with their insides pulled out: shoes and socks were removed, felt carefully and minutely, and prodded, looked in, and searched. Handkerchiefs and necktie were unfolded and vigorously waved. Into a locker for items not allowed went wallet and billfold and all small change, as did tissues and aspirin, comb, key ring and keys.

Briefcase with tape recorders, cassettes, batteries, notepad and notebooks, diary and calendar, two pencils and three pens: all were listed on a manifest and precisely described, then signed for and countersigned. Zips and Velcro-fastened compartments were opened and left exposed. Coded ultraviolet identification marks were stamped on the back of each hand. Time in was noted at 13:29, projected length of stay assessed at three hours. Body search with a metal detector was protracted and precise: stepping through an X-ray arch had to be repeated before two different watchers in turn. The procedure took an hour. "Okay, everything's in order. Have a nice day," the security supervisor said.

Hank Sullivan was a prepossessing man: six feet two inches in height, he weighed two hundred pounds. His ginger beard was bristly, short and carefully trimmed: he had lively steel gray eyes. He wore a barrel-striped clean white sweatshirt with the sleeves rolled up tightly to the tops of his arms and sat with them folded as he sprawled against the wall on an old wooden chair. His voice was deep and resonant and his basso profundo laughter came out frequently and loud. His talk was friendly and animated and his presence filled the white and boxlike room.

Glad to meet you Tony, finally we managed it heh after all of this time? Say just tell me one thing though will you right at the start? Don't mind my curiosity but how much in a year would you reckon that you earned?

Oh fuck come on, no kidding, only that much really? Is that God's truth, that's all? Sweet fucking Jesus when I'm out I make more than that a week. I'd give up if I didn't, so help me God I would, it'd be far too much like work. But then so why'd you go on doing it, why not try something else? I mean do you like it, is it interesting, exciting or what? Pardon me for saying it but you've got to be a nut: I could never have imagined there'd be such crazy folk around. Let me tell you this though, I'm going to drop the idea of trying it myself.

Yeah sure I'll talk with you, like I wrote and said I would. I just hope it's interesting enough for you to feel you want to hear. My story's very simple you see, it's not at all complex, or least not the way I look at it it's not. I'm your ordinary professional criminal and there's plenty around. Some of us successful, some of us aren't, you know how it goes. What's a professional criminal, what does it mean? Well all it is is someone who makes his living out of crime. Like you do with writing, it's more or less like that. You do your writing, I do my crime. Successful or unsuccessful, which one am I? Well successful of course. I must be, I'm here and still alive. I've never thought of giving up, I'm the same way as you: I just can't imagine doing anything else.

My basic facts are few, shall we start with those? You're talking to a man called Hank and his age is fifty-two. He's doing eight terms of imprisonment for life, plus six sentences consecutive totaling three hundred years. The life terms are for shootings in which people got killed, and the fixed sentences are for different offenses like attempted murder, wounding, armed robbery, possession of explosives, robbery with violence, escape, resisting arrest and that kind of stuff. All of it straight though, nothing kinky or weird. Parole is something I'll never ever be given, no matter what, which I guess some guys'd take to mean they'd never get out. Not me though, not me my friend, myself I don't look at it that way. Because for sure if I did, well then I'd be dead.

How do I mean? Well let out and get out, they're two different things. They won't let me out ever, not from the front door, sure I know that. So what I have is the only alternative, you know what I mean? If it can't be the front then that only leaves the back. So escape's my ambition and the planning of it is all that keeps me alive. In twenty years I've made it twice so it's not an impossible dream. I'm not that sort of a man. I mean if I was I'd be frustrated wouldn't I, all disappointed and sour and eaten up inside. But I'm not. I'll get out again one day, there's no doubt about that. Believe me, do, okay?

Go back to the beginning for you, my background and childhood, you want to hear about those? Sure I'll tell you then, it won't take too much time. You see there's nothing to tell. I'm from a white middle-class Catholic family, perfectly ordinary, straight down the line. As a kid I was happy and we weren't rich, but neither were we poor. We lived in a nice home, we were well raised and wanted for nothing or nothing I recall. My father was a production manager at a factory and my mother was a teacher; both of them are dead now, but they were nice people and good. They were very happy with each other, you know how some people are? They believed in family ties and values, and all that kind of thing. I've a brother and two sisters, all older than me. I've not been in contact with any of them since I was young, but as far as I know they've led conventional lives. Both my sisters are married and I couldn't tell you what their names are. That's about all I can think of that there's to say where my family's concerned. They don't really exist for me for practical purposes in any meaningful kind of way now, because that's how it goes.

Schooling, I guess that'd be interesting if I could remember any-thing of it that left any mark but I'm sorry no, I can't. I went to a Catholic high school for boys and the teachers were priests. I wasn't ever beaten or sexually interfered with. There were none of those things went on you sometimes read about, so there's no interest there, just nothing at all. I think I usually got good grades. My life was not unusual and nothing occurred in it for the first ten years I'd say. No one specially influenced me either for good or for bad, you know what I mean?

The fact I was secretive and had an inner life was all that made me any different, I suppose. If you'd met me then you'd never have imag-ined more than anyone else what was happening inside. Exteriors conceal, right? In my case I was amusing myself from the age of ten on with stick-ups and fires. They were like kind of my hobbies, but they were much more than that: for me they were my all-consuming inter-ests would be more correct to say. I guess to some folk that'd be unusual in a way, but if it is it didn't seem so to me. It wasn't my life was dull you know and I wanted to escape from it and fizz it up a bit; I just found it interesting to do those things and watch how people would react. Guns were easy to get like they always are, and the first one I had was like a train set for me, I'd clean it and polish it and look after it like it was a treasure or my very best friend. My very first gun, a Colt .45 automatic, gee I'll never forget that one, I loved it I did. Like the way you remember your first woman, you know how I mean?

The other part intrigued me was the psychology thing: people are always more frightened of a kid with a gun than they are of an adult armed robber, have you ever noticed that? Because they think he's not going to be so reasonable and responsible in the way he handles it like a grown-up would I suppose. Might fire a shot at them for just a trivial thing like moving too quick or something of that sort. There was a cabdriver once I stuck up when I was twelve; he'd pulled in an alley where I'd told him to go, and when I let him see the gun and told him to give me all he'd got, he got almost hysterical with fear. "Don't shoot me, don't shoot me" he went on and on. I had to really make a big effort to try and talk him down. I said "Look buddy I'm not going to shoot you" I said, "just so long as you give me all there is." You know this guy was shitting himself he was so terrified. I mean can you imagine that?

As for those fires, the arson bit I mean, when I first started coming into juvenile institutions and places of that kind, it used to cause so much fucking interest among psychologists and shrinks you wouldn't believe. Very unusual and significant, least that's what they always said. Going to bed with your sister or wanting to fuck your mother, that was ordinary stuff, but a fourteen-year-old who was a serial arsonist, well he really was, he was some special kind of guy. All I did actually was set fire to warehouses and stores and offices and schools and that sort of place. Just for fun you know. But they'd never accept it was that, it always had to be symbolic of something: I found that kind of weird, I really did. One center I was in a psychologist had me write down every single place I'd done. Sixteen as I recall and they divided them in groups: "masculine" and "feminine," "aggressive" and "passive" and some other categories I forget. It was a young woman who done this stuff, and I remember her better than I remember all the shit. She had a real short white overall and a pretty tight little ass, and she'd all the time lean over the table I was sitting at to mark up the blocks. So what I did naturally was I stretched it all out, then while she was arranging all the papers and covering them with marks I'd stand round in back of her and peek up her skirt or look down her front to try and see her tits. A strange kind of occupation for a young girl to have, studying someone like me. But I let her have her fun though, I didn't mind: one of us was normal and the other one was not.

My brain starts to ramble, it's a sign of getting old. I don't think I've any more to tell you about those fires, except how I worked. I read all I could about inflammable substances in the library and experimented making compounds of my own. Oh yeah something else there was which brings us back to psychology again. How it is with fire raisers, do you know about that? They're always supposed to go and watch what they've done, the conflagrations they've caused and that's how most of them get caught, they can't keep away. Well I was well aware of that so I avoided it, every single time: I'd set timing devices made from cheap stolen clocks, and when a fire of mine started I'd be gone far away. I usually went back to the roof of our house; from there you could see, and hear the fire tenders' sirens. That was the best part for me because it meant a success. But if it didn't happen I wouldn't go back to see what was wrong, I'd just write that one off and try another time some place else.

You know I guess the best part of all though was hearing people talk. They sure caused some chattering, those fires of mine did. "They've caught the arsonist," that I often heard, or words to the effect the owner of the premises was responsible himself, he'd done it for insurance because business was bad. You know what people say. How many I did in total I can't properly recall because I never did something stupid like keeping a list. Sixteen I told the psychologist about, but that sure was not them all; twenty-five or thirty say would be nearer the mark in around about a year. And then it all finished and came to an end. How I was caught was real stupid, no doubt at all. How it is when you're young, right, it's always the same? You want to impress some girl, and that's just what I did. I was boasting one night to her it was me who'd set the fires, and she said she didn't believe it, I was trying to pull her leg. So what did I do? I gave her a forecast: I told her wait and see, on the Saturday night I'd set alight a certain store. So when it went up like I said it would, what happened, well anyone could guess: she told her parents what I'd said. The cops were round my place in five minutes flat, and in my room they found things I'd not had time to hide. My parents were pretty shaken by it, especially my dad. He sat me down I remember and he said he knew I hadn't done such things and I must be protecting someone else, like parents always do. Finally he said he'd help me and in every way he could, but only if I'd swear on the Bible to him to tell the honest truth. I said okay I'd do that, and that's what I did: I swore on the word of God that I'd acted entirely on my own, and I guess that made him feel pretty bad. He was a good man by his lights and he just couldn't understand. It taught me a lesson though, the experience I mean and I've tried to remember it since all through my life but with varying success. What it is you'll know it, like every other man: Never trust a dame.

What happened in the end was I was sent to reform school for an indefinite period, which was precisely four years. I'd say they were some of the best of my life. I mixed with guys like myself whose only aim was crime. There was a thousand juvenile offenders there of every kind you could imagine, and a lot I'm sure you couldn't, you know what I mean? That's an experience you know I'd not otherwise have had. It was good, it taught me possibilities and it opened up my eyes. Also it made me tough. You know I've often thought this since, the guys who do their time better are the ones who started early. That I honestly believe, now I've thought it out, which I've just this minute done.

I don't know what was with my parents after that, somehow we seemed to grow apart. They visited a time or two, but I never went back home; it didn't seem to have no point, we sort of lived in different worlds. I'd say from eighteen up I only associated with all my own kind. Funny, things like that, it's the way it often works. I mean some folks you fit with but others you can only say if they hadn't been your relatives you'd never have known them even for a start. Then someone else you meet and it's like you've known them all your life. That was how it was with me and my first serious girl: she was the sister of a guy I was buddy-buddy with in there. We never talked it over or arranged it any way, but as soon as I got out I went to the apartment she had, and I think all we said was "Hi there" before we then went straight to bed. That's the way it should be, so I've always found. Then you know where you are and you won't get surprised by discovering you're with a vegetarian or someone of that kind.

She was a good kid that girl was, I owe a lot to her: she was the person gave me my first proper chance. Sheila her name was or Sheena, something of the kind. She had some Irish in her you know like I do as well, and we were both brought up Catholic, which was another thing—we were ideally suited to each other in most every way there was. She wasn't much of a looker but I don't think you should let that count: what mattered was she had brains, was good with figures and intelligent. She had a job in the central cashier's office of a chain of carpet and furnishing stores, and she knew the days of the month where their different cash drops were made. That was very useful for me because she could point me to all the places where I needed to be, tell me what time the armored truck with the wages in it would arrive and all stuff like that.

Honestly I did, I learned a lot from that girl: not just where and when to make the strikes but how to plan them out so's they looked like they were at random and no one could trace a pattern in them, point a finger, you know? That stuff was very useful for a young guy like me beginning on a criminal career. I think she was hoping one day I'd make a big enough pile for us to retire and settle down. It was sad for her it didn't happen like that. My trouble was you see I had a wandering eye, something I've never come to terms with in my life. I don't attach myself to people, there's too many risks—lays you open to their moods instead of keeping them to yours. Me and her, Sheena or whatever her name was, things were going along very nice and smoothly for a couple of years till she started talking about wanting to settle down. There was nothing else for it: one night I upped and I didn't come back because you don't want discussions, you just make the break like that. Besides women can peach on you, threaten to tell, and that can lead to awkwardness. I've had it happen and it's not very nice. As soon as they say they might, the best thing to do is make for the door.

I'd say on the whole though I've been lucky with my women, they've mostly given me good times. There was one I remember, now she was one of the best, a feisty little girl; only sixteen, fast-legged and sprinty like a quarter horse. Got me to train her how to use a thirty-eight, and she was the sort to go out and pull jobs I myself'd think twice about first. She was some kid she was, red hair and not all that tall, only came up to here. You know what she'd do? What she was good at especially, it was usually hotels. She'd sit in the bar of one and when some guy propositioned her they'd go up to his room. Ten minutes flat and she'd get him stripped naked, down to his drawers. Then she'd take off all her own clothes and get him so dazzled he'd fall on the bed, and when he did that then she'd reach for her purse, pull out her gun and make him give her his last cent. Takes courage to do that you know, for a girl on her own. I used to tell her if she was my daughter I would, I'd feel real proud.

Say you know what Tony, let me tell you something: I'm really enjoying talking to you, it's great to reminisce. Put a new tape in? Sure, go ahead.

Women eh, there was other ones too, plenty in my time. I met a broad once, believe me she was sixty-five, she was a little old granny and she drove a big truck and suggested we go into partnership. Only let me tell you, that's something I've never ever done—take on one other guy and the risk grows three ways. One is he could let you down and not play his part; two he could get injured and captured to follow; three if he is he could try to save his neck by telling what he knows. I'd say to any young guy to always bear that in mind: wherever it's practicable, stay on your own.

Let me tell you an example: The first time I ever came to prison, it wasn't my fault. Me and another guy, we'd held up a security truck that was taking wages to a factory. I'd done all the planning about where exactly we'd stop it which was on a bridge over a canal. Then at the last minute I heard it had four armored guards, not two like I'd been told. I always reckoned I could deal with two when I worked on my own, but four was rather different; you'd need eyes in the back of your head. So what did I do but I took on an assistant, and when the shooting started he took a bullet in his hip. He wasn't wearing body armor like I'd told him he should so of course he was caught. They beat it out of him where I was making for and they had twenty police vehicles and dogs and a helicopter too. They got me in the woods and threw a cordon round it, and all because this guy gave them knowledge so they could work out my route. I had no way out except fire power: in the confrontation I shot more accurately than they did but one against twenty's not fair odds and I surrendered in the end. I gave a good account of myself first, I think I took out a total of four, but I finished up with two life sentences plus two hundred years.

Considering for ten years I'd been working nice and steady and never once being caught, as you can imagine I felt very bitter about that result. I still think if I hadn't had that amateur along, I'd most likely have shaken off pursuit. I've learned my lesson about that, or mostly I have. I don't want to be boastful, but if someone wants to hire my services for something big when I'm out I always lay down strict conditions that they leave me alone to work the way I want to, which means on my own. I won't do nothing for anyone if I have to follow their instructions; they must follow mine.

Another thing is this: I won't do just anything, I always make it plain that there's lines. An obvious one from which I'll never deviate is I'll never hurt a woman, not for any sum at all. I don't know if it means I'm softhearted or what. I've been offered contracts and some of them were big ones, but if it's a woman, then the answer's no. I don't touch females, get somebody else. On the whole though taking individuals out, that's really not my line. I've only done two contract hits in the whole of my life, or three at the most. They're sneaky, know what I mean? I wouldn't ever touch them unless business was real bad; I'd sooner stand up and fight. I don't like killing people when they're not armed.

The excitement, you know, that's the part I like: I'm not the sort goes round shooting at random anyone I see. All of my killings they've all had a purpose, I'm a professional criminal, not a fucking psychopath. Those first two I told you about, I was trying to get away, then the next three again, they were all of men with guns who were moving me to a different state or other to face some more charges. The chances of breaching a maximum security establishment are low because you're outnumbered by the guards, so the best times are when they're moving you. Then the same thing again two years ago, there were just two prison guards. That's only seven? One two thr . . . Oh yeah you're right, so who the hell was . . . yeah wait a minute, I've got it now, the second escape it wasn't three it was four, a state trooper turned up and thought he'd join in. Though I'll be honest with you, there's been a couple of others too that haven't come out and I think they never will. How many in total? Jeez I've no idea, more than ten it must be I guess.

Let me try and tell you how it is. Firstly I don't have to justify myself, there's no need. I guess the way I'd put it would be to say it's like we are at war, me and society I mean. I see myself as a law enforcement officer—only my laws, not yours. Or another way to say it would be there's one set of guys whose uniforms are blue: they try and hang on to things like money and possessions and power. And then there'd be other ones whose uniforms are green: they want to get a slice of things themselves too. The one way they'll not do it is work from nine through five so they have to think of other ways. I've chosen one which I thoroughly enjoy: it's plotting and scheming and working out a strategy, then putting it into action and seeing if it works. And again I'm not boasting in saying this to you because it's true: I've been successful a hundred times more often than I've ever been caught for, that's certainly a fact. We're cleverer than we're given credit for, people like me, we certainly are.

I'm a professional criminal, and I take pride in my trade. An amateur, you see, he's not like that at all. How I'd define him would be a guy who makes a quick hit and relies on his luck for the amount of cash he gets: could be a few hundred bucks, might be nothing at all. But for me I need to know first what the amount is's involved, and the amount of risk I'll take's got to be commensurate with the financial reward. If it looks like it's going to be a combat situation I wouldn't go in underarmed; always at least I've got to have an automatic rifle, two pistols and at least some hand grenades. "Armed to the teeth" would be the phrase.

Obviously if it's something big other guys are going to try and stop me, right? They'll go as far as they think's necessary to do that, including killing me of course. Then I'm saying in return that to stop me that's what they'll have to do, and if they try, then I'm going to try and kill them first. That's common sense, okay? But don't get me wrong like I said before: I wouldn't kill anyone unless it was strictly necessary to get what I wanted or it was my life or theirs.

Would I ever kill you, you want an honest answer to that? Well the answer is no, probably not. I can't envisage the situation arising can you, where it would be necessary? I mean if you were a guard here and I had a gun, if I wanted your key I'd ask you for it. I'd say "Give me your key." And if you were sensible about it as I think you would be and did what I asked and stood to one side, then of course I wouldn't kill you, because there wouldn't be a need. On the other hand though if you crazily decided you wouldn't give me the key and went for your gun, then of course I'd blow your fucking head in. I'd have to wouldn't I, otherwise you might do me harm? That answer your question, do you understand? Good: no hard feelings I hope.

Oh boy Tony I've enjoyed this you know, I truly have. It's been like the kind of conversation you usually have with yourself, know what I mean? Good luck with the book.

VI

VICTIMS

None of the people in this section knows, is known to, or has any connection with those in the previous sections of the book.

I WISH I'D NEVER HAPPENED

CLARENE DEAN

orty-seven, she was hollow voiced and thin; there were black shadows like bruises under her eyes. Her scarlet lipstick made her thin-lipped mouth look like a long slash across her chalk-white skin.

It's ten years now since my daughter was murdered: she was twenty, nearly twenty-one. They say time makes it easier don't they, but it's not, at least it's not easier for me. There's never a day I don't cry about it. That's a photo of her on the cabinet there; I've one in every room. She was training as a nurse.

I didn't idolize Elaine, we weren't always on good terms as a matter of fact. She was living with a man, he was black, I didn't greatly care for that. I hoped for someone better for her, I suppose all mothers do. But he was a bad lot, he got her into drugs and he didn't have a regular job. I didn't approve and we had regular big fights. She said she loved him and she wouldn't ever give him up. If she had she'd still be alive. He stabbed her thirty-four times and left her body in the rain down a culvert on an empty lot. Jealousy, they said.

It doesn't get any easier to talk about. I live the memory of her every day and every night. Excuse me a moment, I've some pills here in my purse. Come on now Clarene, come on.

Anniversaries are the worst; I dread each one. Her birthday, Thanksgiving, Halloween I remember when she was a kid—I remember them all. It's often times like those something strange happens,

215

like I imagine I see her across the street. One year I was so certain it was her I ran after a young woman and caught her arm. When she turned around all I could say was "Oh I'm so sorry" and I burst into tears. I don't know what she thought; she must have thought I was a mad person escaped from somewhere I think.

No one understands really; I mean how could they I mean? A year or two afterwards, I used to go to church for a while. Now I don't go anymore, I don't believe there is a God. I'm not saying if there was he wouldn't have let Elaine die like that, it's just I didn't find any comfort in religion, I can't believe there's a purpose to things or life makes any sense. Some people feel differently, perhaps I hadn't enough faith. When Elaine's murderer left her body where he did, there was no dignity or decency in that kind of death. I blame God for it, she deserved better than that.

My husband and my son, both went to court and they told me when he gave his evidence the murderer broke down. He pleaded guilty and he said they'd quarreled and he loved her and he was sorry and it was all through the drugs. I asked them if they believed him. They both said yes. But he stabbed her thirty-four times and he tried to hide her body and then he ran. He should have turned himself in. No one asked him why he didn't. The judge accepted his mitigation statement and gave him life. One day he'll have parole.

What I'd like people to understand is I don't think it should be looked at like that. The murderer of my daughter didn't only murder her, he murdered everyone she knew connected with her life. It finished my own marriage: after three years my husband left me for someone else. My son married and he's living in Vermont. We don't see each other, him and his wife have two kids and I don't like her, she said life must go on. Okay so that's okay for them. He sends me a little money and so does my husband now and then.

Sometimes I think I'll take a job and change my name. I wish I'd never happened: if I hadn't none of this ever would. I wouldn't let myself be involved with anyone again—I feel that would be like betraying Elaine. If I'd been closer with her she might still be alive. It's only in me she's living now, that's all of her that's left.

I don't believe in the death penalty, all that is is revenge. But I feel the man who murdered Elaine and ended her life should have his own life ended too: he ought to be kept locked up for the rest of his life and told he wouldn't ever be paroled. If you take a life of another person you should forfeit what's left of your own. However long it is he sits there he knows all he has to do is wait and one day he'll come out. He has another life to look forward to which is more than he gave Elaine.

I don't drink but can I offer you a coffee maybe or something?

A SOMEONE TO
FOCUS ON

GORDON WARRINGTON

*B*lack, tall and heavily built he was in his sixties and had an open friendly smile. He spoke quietly and with dignity, wearing a business suit and clasping together the long fingers of his hands.

What I always say to folks is slowly: you know, very very slowly, that's the only way it comes. You don't get over the shock and hurt of it in a week or in a year. You can't, believe me, there's no way you can, and you never ever will. Only as time passes, the dominance of it gets less, you put it in proportion. But it takes a long long time.

Brett was my only son and it's six years now he was killed. He was a policeman. I'd been in the force myself the whole of my life and that made me proud. My wife didn't like it and our two daughters didn't like it either that he was; they said one was enough and they tried to persuade him to go in some different direction. But he felt like I did that citizens have duties and some of us must do something to check the violence of our lives. But in twenty-five years no one ever once tried to kill me and I never fired my gun. For Brett it was six years only and then some thug shot him dead. It was in the street in broad daylight and he was trying to stop a wages truck heist and was answering a call.

In my time I'd done it often as part of my job to have to go see someone and tell them one of their loved ones had lost his life and wasn't coming home. I didn't like doing it but you have to get inured. When I was the one who opened the door myself and saw an officer in uniform saying he was sorry but he had bad news that was the first time I learned how it really felt for them.

The culprit's trial took three weeks and I attended every day. My wife couldn't take it so I was there on my own. It made me angry to watch. The judge he was an elderly white man, and the man who'd murdered my son was white; the prosecuting attorneys and the defending attorneys were all white too, every single one. Finally the judge stopped the trial on the grounds of insufficient evidence, so the guy walked. No one'll ever convince me there wasn't a certain element of racism to it, you know? It was their society my boy Brett gave his life for after all.

When I told my wife the verdict she took to her bed for eight months and two days. Both our daughters offered to have us live with them and their families, but we didn't think we should burden them that way. Then one morning I came home from walking the dog in the park and my wife wasn't there. I feared the worst but ten minutes or so after she reappeared. She'd got up and dressed herself and gone shopping at the mall: she'd had her hair done and a facial and bought herself some clothes. I took her on my knee and we wrapped our arms around each other and sat for half an hour and cried.

What we do now is give a lot of our time to a support group for others like ourselves. It has over one hundred attenders, some of them are regular and some of them are not. My wife's the treasurer and I'm the secretary. It's one hell of a lot of work but I'd say to anyone in our position they should do something similar: give as much time as you can to helping others because that's the best way to help yourself. Someone else to think about; you're not spending so much time thinking about the murderer either, which I think a lot of people do. He has a useful purpose, he's a someone to focus on, someone to blame, but that kind of thinking's sterile, it won't bring back the person you've lost. You've got to try and redirect your feelings and help others to do the same.

There's not a day my wife and I don't talk together about Brett and mention his name. But we try and keep it positive, remember the good times we had with him and the funny little things about him no one else knows. We have twenty-eight years' memories of him to choose from, so we never run short.

I don't agree with capital punishment, first because it isn't a deterrent to the sort of person who killed my son, and second because I know from my lifetime's work that mistakes can be made and they sometimes are. I don't believe it personally, but it could be so in Brett's case there wasn't sufficient evidence absolutely to nail the guy: if there had been, I think he should have been put away for a long long time. Sometimes I wonder what I'd do if we ever came face-to-face, him and me. I don't know if I would, but I like to think I'd ignore him and walk on by.

YOU ONLY GOT
ONE MOM

JIMMY CHENEY

*H*e sat on a bench in the park, sticking his legs out in front of him stiffly and staring at his feet. He wore baggy navy shorts, a crumpled brown sweatshirt, and a baseball cap with "Giants" on it perched sideways on his head. Round shouldered and fat, he was small for his age.

I'm fourteen. I live with my grandparents on Twenty-third Street and I go to St. Joseph's Senior High. My mom was murdered when I was seven. I don't remember much about her except she was nice, and me and my sister loved her a lot. She and my dad were divorced: I don't know why, I guess they didn't get along so good. My grandma says she'll tell me about it one day and then I'll understand how it was. I didn't like my stepfather but I didn't know him very much: he was the person murdered her and he was sent to jail for life. I had a letter from him once asking me would I go see him because he wanted us to get to know each other; I didn't want to get to know him so I didn't send a reply.

It's not easy when you're a kid knowing what to say when other kids ask you about your mom and how she died. My grandma said I should say she was killed in an air crash or something like that. I think a lot of them would know that isn't the truth. Nobody's ever said anything direct to me about it though. I was thinking about her in class the other day and I started to cry. The teacher took me outside the classroom and put her arms around me and said it was okay if I wanted to go home. Her name's Miss Marshall: I think she definitely knows and I think the other teachers do too. Why the other kids would make fun of me is I suppose because that's how kids are. One boy there has a sister that's dead and some of the bigger pupils sometimes shout at him about it and make fun of him and that.

I go to church and they have there what's called a counseling group for children on Friday night. About twelve go and we meet once a week for an hour with Reverend Birtwhistle and his wife. If you've got a problem like your parents are divorced or your pa's an alcoholic or something you can talk about it and tell the others how you feel. If you want to you can cry even if you're a boy and no one will give you a hard time. Reverend Birtwhistle begins with a prayer and then he says a problem shared is a problem halved and asks who'd like to start. The last two times he's said it he's looked at me. I haven't said anything yet because I don't like to. When the others talk it's always about their parents' marriages busting up or someone in their family's died. I don't think anyone else there besides me's had their mother murdered. It makes me feel I'm on my own.

I believe in Heaven and all that, and I know my mom's not really dead: she's up there looking down and watching out for me. When I play baseball and I get a good hit, one that goes real high in the air I say "That one's for you, Mom." I know she'll be proud of me because it'll make me special for her like she is for me.

It makes me sad I don't have her anymore. The guy who killed her is in jail and he's still alive: he's sitting there eating his food and watching TV which she can't do. She can't ever come back to earth again, yet the people in court've never come and asked me what I thought about it. You only got one mom so she wasn't so special for them as she was for me. I think they should have given me a gun and let me kill him if I wanted to. It's my opinion he should have had the death penalty without any argument, as everybody like him should.

That would tell people they can't commit murders and get away with it, they will pay for it with their own life. If you have a dog and it kills another dog it gets put to death, and that's how it should be with people if they kill another one. It says in the Bible there should be an eye for an eye and a tooth for a tooth and I agree with that.

COULD ANYONE REALLY
SAY THAT?

GINNY MASON

*D*ressed *in a black jacket and matching skirt, she had a tur-
quoise blouse and fashionably coiffured short fair hair. She
talked quietly, eating a crispbread and an orange, sipping a
glass of California chablis as she lunched at her office desk.*

I'm thirty-six and I'm the art director of this magazine. I've been
here ten years, I'm married and my husband and I have two children,
a boy of eight and a six-year-old girl.

My younger brother Malcolm was murdered twelve years ago
when he was twenty; I was then twenty-four. He worked in the cash
office of a loan company. He'd been with them six months and the
pay was good, and he and his fiancée were planning their wedding.
Our father had died two years before, and between us we'd settled our
mother in a small nearby apartment of her own. At that time I was
living with Neil who's now my husband, and Malcolm shared a house
with a young man his own age he'd been at college with who was his
best friend.

We saw a lot of each other, mostly at weekends. Sundays Malcolm
usually would bring Ma over to Neil and my place for lunch or we'd
go out to the country club. Sundays were always our special family
days and we'd all tell one another what we'd been doing in the week.
Ma always really looked forward to what she called our Sunday get-
togethers. Her health wasn't good, especially since when she lost Pa,
but she went to the library a lot and read a lot of magazines and

watched TV and she always took an interest in what was going on in the world. What Malcolm could do like no one else was really make her laugh: he always exaggerated about things that had happened to him or weird people he'd met. She knew it, but sometimes I'd look at her when she was listening to him and she was smiling; he was what they call the apple of her eye. I used to get a little bit jealous of him when I was younger but I was always Daddy's girl so I guess at times he must have felt the same about me.

The morning it happened I got a phone call where I then worked; it was Malcolm's office manager and he asked me to go over quick. He said there'd been a serious accident and Malcolm'd been badly hurt. He said he couldn't give me any more details over the phone and they didn't know how to contact Ma. I couldn't take it in at first when he told me when I got there. Two masked men had burst in and fired shots at the ceiling and told everyone to lie facedown on the floor. They made the manager hand over the safe keys to them. Malcolm thought they couldn't fully see him and he tried to reach the alarm button under one of the desks. One of the men shot him three times in the chest from as far away from him as I am from you and he killed him instantly. Then they panicked and ran out. The cops wanted to know where Ma lived so they could go round and tell her, but I asked them to take me and let me do it. It wasn't a thing I'd wish on anyone having to do. She died the following year.

The two men who did it weren't caught for three months: they were captured trying to do the same thing in South Dakota I think it was. Nobody knows whether they did other robberies and killings in between. It took more than a year before they were tried. They were both given death sentences and went to the chair. I read about it in the papers but I don't remember their names.

I don't feel anything about it much really, I've built up my own life and family since. I know what it did to Ma and I'm sad my young brother who'd never done any harm to anyone was murdered in cold blood by two men he didn't even know and who didn't know him. I've no pity for them; I never even think about them. That they didn't deserve to die, could anyone really say that? If it had been me I'd have thrown the switch to kill them without a second thought.

All the stuff about trying to understand murderers is total shit, who gives a fuck? You kill someone, you kill someone and that's all there is: if someone kills you for doing it that's what you deserve.

WALKING A LONELY CORRIDOR

MARGARET FERGUSON

A *pale lilac track suit and beige slippers; rimless steel spectacles and pale blue eyes. She blinked nervously while she talked, lighting a cigarette, cupping a plastic coffee mug in her frail thin hands. She was fifty-seven, with thinning gray hair.*

I have a daughter called Susan and three lovely little grandchildren, but they live in New York; they come and visit twice a year. It's usually Easter and Thanksgiving, they stay with us a week each time. Fortunately they get on with my husband and he's very fond of them so everything's okay. My first husband, Susan's father, he and I divorced when she was three. He lives in Paris, France, with his second wife with whom he has four children. He writes occasionally to her, but not to our son Bill, who's Susan's elder brother, never to him at all.

I came here to live seven years ago. I like it and I've made quite a few friends. Well more acquaintances I should say. Susan's father's fairly generous over alimony so I have no problems financially, I get along. It's not exactly a mansion where I live as you see, but I have my little car out in the driveway there and I've really all I need. Tuesdays and Thursdays I go to Bluebell Valley which is the old folks' home: I play the piano and we have a sing-along and I think a lot of the residents appreciate that. With one or two of them I've gotten to be real friends.

Maybe I'll stay here the rest of my time. I hope so; we've moved house three times now the last ten years. Fred, he's my husband, he's coming up for retirement soon and I know he'd like us to settle. He's been good about us moving in the past: he's always said the important thing's I should be happy about where we were. I feel I owe it him to let him stay in one place now where he can put down roots, enjoy his golf and stuff like that, specially since he's been so good about Bill who's not even his own son I mean. A lot of men wouldn't have been that way. Also he takes three or four days off from work when I go visit Bill. It's a drive seven hundred miles there and seven hundred miles back and that's a long way to travel for someone Fred's age.

My son Bill is doing two natural life sentences for rape and murder of a seventeen-year-old girl. He did it nineteen years ago and they say he's no chance ever of parole. I don't want to say anything to the detriment of the girl or make any kind of excuses for Bill: I never have. I guess like other mothers who've had something of this kind happen in their lives I feel guilty about it to some extent myself—like if I hadn't done this or that or had raised him differently it wouldn't have occurred. Me and his father divorced when he was seven and I brought him and Susan up on my own and I can see all the things I did wrong. Even remarrying again: I feel I was selfish about that, putting my own happiness first. But then I have to say that even if Fred's only his stepfather and not his real parent, no one could have cared for Bill more or had a better relationship with him. Certainly his own father didn't, he abandoned him and went off with someone else younger and prettier than me. I'm sorry, I shouldn't have said that, it sounds bitter, like I'm trying to put the blame on him.

Bill had been away from home two years, then one day I had this letter from him written from jail in Nebraska saying he was waiting to go for trial. I had to read it six times before I could take in what he was saying, which was he was going to plead guilty because he was. I thought there must be a mistake somewhere and Fred took me to see him and it was like Bill was a stranger. He said I should forget about him, he knew what his sentences would be and there was no point me seeing him anymore. The first year or two he was incarcerated I was tempted to, to be honest I have to say that, I felt I owed it to Fred and Susan to put Bill out of my life. I talked with both of them about it and they both said the same thing: no matter what he did you can't abandon your own son. Maybe without them saying it I would have, I can't really tell.

I go see him twice a year and we write regularly once a month. What worries me most about it is other people finding out. I did tell a neighbor once who I thought would understand. I said it was in confidence but she told other people: I know from how they looked at me in the supermarket or the street, and no one asked me into their homes for coffee anymore. It's like they think you've some kind of unspeakable disease. It was the same for Susan, they wouldn't let their children talk with her. I couldn't take any more of it after a while and Fred agreed we'd move.

This has happened three times now. I've learned my lesson, I've never told anyone else, I don't trust people anymore. What's it got to do with them anyway? You live your life within limits like this; you don't let anyone inside of them and get close to you, it's like walking a lonely corridor.

I'm grateful neither Fred nor Susan ever tells anyone else. Susan hasn't told her children, that I know for sure, and she says she's not going to until they're a lot older than they are. She may have mentioned it to her husband, but if she has he's good about it, he doesn't look at me when we see them as if he knows. If Bill hadn't written to me and said he'd met you and hoped I'd talk with you, you wouldn't have known either would you? If you'd met me some place I don't think you'd have guessed right? Good, no.

ACKNOWLEDGMENTS

When any idea for a book begins to form in my mind, it has now become almost standard practice for me to talk it over with my friend Dr. Anthony Storr and to ask his advice about whether to do it and how: and over the years, no person has ever been more helpful to me in suggesting relevant matters to be considered, paths of thought to be explored, and possible dangers to try to avoid. And, most important, he has always been ready to tell me of other people I should get in touch with as well, for further discussion and possible assistance. It is in a small attempt at recognition and thanks for this friendship and encouragement that I have at last dedicated a book to him. His modesty will make him minimize the importance of his own contributions to my work, but I am glad now to have the opportunity to say why his friendship has been so supportive to me, and his ideas have been so influential on me, for so many years.

Nor could this book have been produced without an enormous amount of help from many other people as well. I spent as long or longer in correspondence and discussions before beginning it than I did in the subsequent interviewing, traveling, and transcribing for it, lengthy and protracted though that was. In England, Dr. Roger Hood at the Centre for Criminological Research at the University of Oxford provided me with much most useful information about the American criminal justice system as well as a list of names of people to write to initially about the project: his help and the use of his name opened many doors, and I am profoundly grateful to him. So too am I to

Professor Ken Pease, Reader in Criminology at the University of Manchester, and also again as always to Professor Terence Morris of the London School of Economics.

In America, innumerable people gave me unstinted help and advice. Professor Anthony Amsterdam and his aide Michael D'Amelio at New York University Law School were never too busy even at particularly busy times for themselves to give attention to an endless series of questions from me. Professor Norval Morris of the University of Chicago Law School, Professor Michael Radelet of the University of Florida, Professor Sean McConville of the University of Illinois, and Professor Rob Johnson of the American University in Washington, were also of very great help: without exception all went to considerable trouble to advise and assist me and share generously their connections and knowledge of systems and methods of approach.

In New York, my contact with the Fortune Society was particularly fruitful. There is nothing like this organization that I know of in England. It is a large drop-in advice center for those recently or immediately out of jail, but far more than that. It operates from a two-floor suite of offices and often about a hundred people, some voluntary workers and some professionals, work as social workers and counselors there. They spend vast amounts of time and energy in face-to-face or group encounters with those rejects of respectable society who have been designated as "criminal": a multitude of whom daily in New York alone have been ejected from incarceration back into a hostile and disorientating environment without help or preparation, and are expected to rehabilitate themselves and refrain from further criminal activity. How they should do it, or to whom they should turn for help, they neither know nor are told. Having no choice therefore, many return to their previous neighborhoods and acquaintances and lives, in which criminal behavior was and still is their daily activity.

At the Fortune Society, if they are lucky enough to come into contact with it, they will be offered alternatives. The first is acceptance as human beings with rights and dignities like others; secondly, they will find readiness by other individuals like themselves many of whom have in the past been convicted offenders, to give help, support, advice, and assistance in beginning the painful process of rethinking their lives and attitudes and goals. Third, they will have there constant access to expert advisers and counselors; and fourth, and perhaps most important, they will be given "thinking space" in which to meditate or discuss with others, without moral disapproval, their often outrageous offenses against society's codes and be offered the fostering of any flickering flame that may still remain inside them to encourage them to change their way of life.

That there should be such a helping haven in the middle of noisy, dirty, and self-absorbed Manhattan is little short of miraculous. And that it is there and continues to exist is almost entirely due to the vision, pragmatism, energy, and dedication of its director, JoAnne Page, a spur and reenergizer to all who come in contact with her. She was prolifically generous in spirit to me, and in practical matters such as introductions, suggestions, and the making of contacts on my behalf she was tireless. My indebtedness to her cannot adequately be expressed.

Among many others who gave me encouragement, assistance, and support outside of New York were Betsy Bernat of the National Prison Project; Janet Welch of Offender Aid and Restoration in Fairfax, Virginia; Stewart Taylor; Gail Smith of Chicago Legal Aid to Incarcerated Mothers; Sharon Smolik of Bedford Hills Correctional Facility; Scott Christianson, deputy director of Parole Operations at the New York State Division of Parole; Assistant Warden Frank Mardavich of Nottoway Correction Center; Parole Officer Richard Mooney of Hempstead Parole Office; Paul Council of the Fortune Society; Hugh Wallace of Wilmington, Delaware; Joe Galowski; Thea Du Bow; Mary Nelson of the Chicago Prison Action Committee; Penny Ryder of Ann Arbor; Jean Auldridge; Keith Nelson; Alan Lefebvre at Graterford Prison, Pennsylvania; Maria Modica of the Victims' Services Agency; Wilbur Smith in Nebraska; and Edward McBain.

Wilbert Rideau, a convicted murderer who has so far spent over thirty years of a life sentence in the Louisiana State Penitentiary at

Angola (and whose story does not appear in this book), was a friendly fount of knowledge and good advice and provided many contacts. So, too, did several other incarcerated offenders in prisons in California, Delaware, Maryland, and Colorado, on condition they would not be named and no specifics would be given about them. CARE, a group of nationwide voluntary workers with and for offenders, provided much help to me too; in particular I am indebted to Charlie and Pauline Sullivan in Washington, D.C., and Wendell Brown of the chapter of Lifelong Care in Boston. Others I must thank for favors large and small include Joan Morrison, Hilda Collins, and Valery Yancey of the New York Law School Housing Office.

In England at my publishers, HarperCollins, Richard Johnson has been all that an author could ask—sympathetic in times of ill health and always encouraging, supportive, and patient—and his colleague Robert Lacey has my profound thanks for his meticulous work in preparation of the final manuscript. In New York William Strachan of Henry Holt has been most understanding and considerate as our working relationship has developed; and in London my agent, Gill Coleridge, has again as always been a constant friend and adviser. Linda Ginn has as usual performed prodigious feats of accuracy and speed in the preparation of transcripts and typescripts; and I also owe thanks to John McCormick of Dunwich for his advice about American usage and terminology, to John Lynham for diminishing my ignorance of the art and work of Billie Holiday, and to Janet Goddard of J. A. Whitehouse, who provided swift and accurate mathematical information by exercising skills totally beyond my comprehension. And also I am particularly grateful to my friend Mary Loudon for pointing out to me that the observation about a journey of a thousand miles beginning with a single step was in fact made not by Confucius, but by Lao-Tsze (c. 604 B.C.).

Of course there is no way I can adequately express my gratitude to the people who agreed to my interviewing them and whose descriptions of themselves and their lives and their offenses constitute the book. They endured my persistent questioning bravely and patiently, speaking frankly of things that frequently caused them great pain to recall. For doing it, they have in equal measure both my thanks and my respect.

Finally, as I've said on previous occasions, I do not know how I can properly thank my wife, Margery, for her indomitable companionship and sharing concern whenever I embark on a book journey. She traveled everywhere with me in America, spent endless hours sitting patiently waiting outside prisons while I was inside them, looked after all my material comforts, bolstered my flagging spirits, and guided my errant navigation as we drove from one place to another in the United States. Without her constant presence and supportive affection, as with so many of my others this book could not have been produced.